a daughter	Lucy
died an infant	1782-1784

Mary Jefferson	Benjamin Franklin	Meriwether Lewis	George Wythe
1803-1876	1808-1871	1810-1836	1818-1867
unmarried	*married*	*married*	*married*
	Sarah Champ Carter	Elizabeth Martin	Mary Pope

James Madison	Septimia Anna
1806-1834	1814-1887
unmarried	*married*
	David S. Meikleham

To the Girls and Boys

To the Girls and Boys

BEING THE DELIGHTFUL, LITTLE-KNOWN LETTERS OF THOMAS JEFFERSON TO AND FROM HIS CHILDREN AND GRANDCHILDREN

selected, with historical notes, by

Edward Boykin

ILLUSTRATED

FUNK & WAGNALLS COMPANY, INC.
New York

PREFACE

I have often wondered why the fascinating letters of Thomas Jefferson to his daughters and his grandchildren—and theirs to him—have apparently been slighted by biographers and other writers.

To this correspondence Jefferson committed many of his celebrated observations on life, love, politics, morality, and education. Yet never has the correspondence between Jefferson and the young folks of his family been published in a single volume of its own.

Jefferson was—and is—a massive, vibrant figure in the history of the nation. Historians have explored and reexplored every facet of his political techniques and philosophies, his achievements and his career; by comparison they seem to have neglected the dearest of all that made life worthwhile (for him, at least): his children, their children, and the strands of ink that bound them to him when they were apart.

On the shelves of our major libraries one can find several editions of Jefferson's collected letters and papers, beginning with the four-volume *Memoir, Correspondence and Miscellanies, from the Papers of Thomas Jefferson,* edited by his grandson, Thomas Jefferson Randolph, in 1829. The newest of these editions, as definitive as research and money can make it, is still emerging from the Princeton University press. This current edition contemplates approximately fifty volumes eventually. Yet the large collections of Jefferson's letters, by their very nature, must bury, amid hundreds of letters and papers of every description, the correspondence with the two daughters he loved so greatly. And as for that with the grandchildren, who filled his maturer years with affection

that amounted to adoration, these massive volumes hardly scratch the surface. When one considers that the sixteenth volume of the current edition has only reached the year 1791, the birth year of Jefferson's first grandchild, it is obvious that years must elapse before this project reaches not only much of the correspondence with his children, but all of that with his grandchildren.

The letters that appear herein reveal the famous statesman in a little-known role: that of a father anxious for the well-being of his motherless, teen-age daughters from whom he was so frequently separated by the exigencies of nation-building, and of a devoted grandfather, who knew how to reach the heart of a child with a goose-quill pen. Most of the correspondence with his grandchildren found in this book is unpublished up to now. The charm of it speaks for itself.

Often playful, sometimes preachy, occasionally scolding, frequently filled with longing to shuck off the tribulations of politics and public office, Jefferson's letters to his daughters were nevertheless flecked with sage advice and simple recipes for their health, comfort, and pleasure. Never was he too busy with affairs of state to indite a letter to them or to the small folk, who, in later years, overran Monticello—letters he sealed with "Kisses," "Tenderest love," and other endearments.

Jefferson's large, expansive family orbited around his idolized figure. Well might he, at the age of seventy-seven, write to Maria Cosway, the love of his life in Paris so long ago, "Among these I live like a partriarch of old." His family entourage included, first of all, his daughter Martha, her husband, Thomas Mann Randolph, Jr., and their numerous progeny, who were virtually permanent residents at Monticello, although their nominal home was Edgehill, four miles across the valley; and his younger daughter, Maria, her husband, John Wayles Eppes, and their small son, Francis. Much of Maria's time after her marriage was spent at her husband's home, Eppington, though she died at Monticello.

On visits home from the successive seats of government—New York, Philadelphia, and Washington—Jefferson urged Martha and her children to live under his own mountaintop rooftree, and even more strongly when the grandchildren began to enliven his household. After his presidential term of office ended in 1809, the Randolphs lived almost continuously at Monticello.

The Randolph offspring were fun-loving, gifted youngsters. Jefferson was never so happy as when his home rang with their shrill, excited voices. He reveled in having them around him, teaching them, playing games with them, sharing with them the secrets of nature he had learned as a boy roaming the nearby mountains, working with them in the flower garden, holding after-dark sessions with them on the lawn while unfolding the mysteries and beauties of the stars. He had a way with small folk. He seemed to divine the secret longings of the little girls and the ambitions of the small boys—and to know how to make them come true.

His grandchildren numbered twelve: eleven Randolphs and one Eppes. By 1818 his older daughter, Martha, had given birth to eleven children, six girls and five boys (seven of whom lived until after the Civil War). They were: Anne Cary, born in 1791; Thomas Jefferson, 1792; Ellen Wayles, 1796; Cornelia Jefferson, 1799; Virginia Jefferson, 1801; Mary Jefferson, 1803; James Madison, 1806; Benjamin Franklin, 1808; Meriwether Lewis, 1810; Septimia, 1814; George Wythe, 1818. The last of these, George Wythe Randolph, was destined to become Secretary of War of the Confederate States. The late-arrivals, four boys, were named by Jefferson for his friends, James Madison, Benjamin Franklin, Meriwether Lewis, and George Wythe. Jefferson's correspondence with his grandchildren was confined largely to Martha's first four children, three girls and a boy, and to Francis Eppes, only surviving child of his daughter Maria.

Others of the Jefferson circle were his widowed sister, Martha Carr—the "Aunt Carr" of these letters—and her six children whom he welcomed to Monticello as his own. She had married Jefferson's best friend, Dabney Carr, whose untimely death left a lifelong vacancy in Jefferson's affections. In gratitude and love the Carr family warmly repaid his kindness. To these should be added Jefferson's youngest sister, Anna (Mrs. Hastings Marks), whose lengthy visits to Monticello qualified her as a semipermanent resident. But this was what Jefferson wanted: his whole family around him.

The letters used in this book are selected mostly from his correspondence during his public career as a member of the Continental Congress, minister plenipotentiary to France, Secretary of State, Vice President and President of the United States. They begin in 1783, the year after the heartbreaking death of his wife. He had just taken his seat with the Virginia delegation in the Congress.

I have not attempted to tell a running story with the letters, though they are linked with explanatory settings and biographical material. After a fashion, they convey the story of Jefferson's private and public life from 1783 to the end.

TO THE GIRLS AND BOYS contains a number of letters to and from Jefferson's daughters not generally known. Most of the letters from his grandchildren have never been printed be-

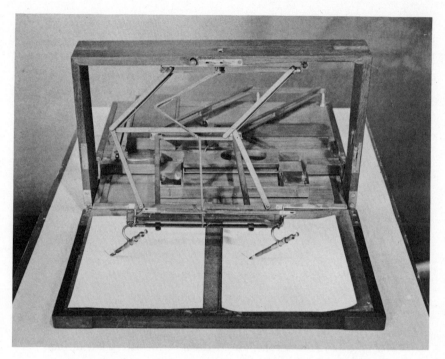

Jefferson invented this polygraph to make duplicates of his letters.

fore. Jefferson's correspondence with the girls and boys of the family has not attracted too much notice. But Jefferson apparently felt otherwise. He kept every scrap of their correspondence, even their childhood scrawls.

Over the years Jefferson's letters have suffered dispersion and loss in many forms. His "letter books" are replete with entries of letters written and received but now vanished. He kept copies of most of his letters, using quill, letterpress, and a polygraph of his own invention. Actually, he kept an indexed record (it runs to six hundred and fifty-six pages) of every letter he wrote or received from 1783 to 1826. As with letters of other founders of the Republic, long-hidden Jefferson letters have a way of cropping up when least expected, even after the experts had about decided there were no more extant. Not too long ago a dusty, discarded old desk in the U. S. Senate attic in the Capitol disgorged a package of yellowed papers among which were autographs of Jefferson, Washington, and John Adams.

This book does not include all the extant correspondence with Jefferson's daughters, but it does include a sizable part of his extant correspondence with his grandchildren.

Charlottesville   E. B.
Virginia

Note to Reader. No liberties have been taken with Jefferson's felicitous diction. Whenever the letters of Jefferson are available in the original, I have reproduced them faithfully. Jefferson had a style and orthography distinctly his own. He used capital letters sparingly, seldom beginning a sentence with one; he often dispensed with periods at the end of sentences. When the original letters are long lost, I have, of course, had to rely on published versions. Jefferson's first major biographer was Henry S. Randall, whose three-volume "life" was published in 1857. In quoting Jefferson's letters, Randall—just as Jefferson's other editors would do—capitalized and repunctuated at will. As for the young folks, their letters, too, are printed here actually as they wrote them—when the originals were obtainable, that is.

A few points of style. To indicate that omissions have been inherited from a previous editor, a series of asterisks has been used. I, myself, being reluctant to tantalize the reader, have included many an ambiguous or even dull paragraph. When, however, I have deleted material that could be of little interest to the reader, I have indicated such omissions by a series of periods.

CONTENTS

ACKNOWLEDGMENTS

Foremost among the institutions to which the writer is indebted for permission to draw on their magnificent Jefferson manuscript collections in the preparation of this book are: the Alderman Library of the University of Virginia, in Charlottesville, Virginia, and the Massachusetts Historical Society in Boston, Massachusetts.

To Anne Freudenberg, Acting Curator of Manuscripts, and to Elizabeth Ryall, Assistant in Manuscripts, for the Alderman Library, the writer extends his hearty thanks for unfailing courtesies and great assistance. To Stephen T. Riley, Director of the Massachusetts Historical Society, the writer is likewise indebted for permission to draw on much of the correspondence of Jefferson with his grandchildren. Without the cooperation of these three this book would hardly have been possible.

To the Library of Congress the writer is indebted for many favors, including access to the greatest of Jeffersonian collections and permission to use material therefrom. Helpful indeed were the Henry E. Huntington Library, in San Marino, California; the University of North Carolina Library; the Virginia State Library; the National Archives in Washington, D.C.; the J. Pierpont Morgan Library in New York; and the Missouri Historical Society at St. Louis.

The writer also acknowledges his indebtedness to the Thomas Jefferson Memorial Foundation that owns and maintains the home of the great patriot. To William S. Hildreth, President of the Foundation, to James A. Bear, Jr., Curator of Monticello, and to W. Curtis Thacker, Superintendent of Monticello, the author is deeply grateful for permission to take photographs within the mansion.

The writer's thanks are also acknowledged to John R. Campbell, Assistant Information Officer of the American Embassy at Paris; to the New York Historical Society, in New York City; to the Yale University Art Gallery, in New Haven, Connecticut; to Mr. Arthur Rotch of Milton, Massachusetts; and especially to Mrs. Page Kirk of Charlottesville, herself a descendant of Thomas Jefferson. And further to Ed Roseberry of Charlottesville for his fine photography work.

Thanks are also due Virginia Corey and Betty Hoskins of the Photostat Laboratory of the Alderman Library for many fine favors. The writer should like to commend his excellent amanuensis, Marjorie Wolfrey, of Charlottesville, for her prompt and indefatigable assistance.

To the Girls and Boys

I

Martha Jefferson

1 7 7 2 - 1 8 3 6

*"It produces great praise to a lady to
spell well"*

In one of Thomas Jefferson's notebooks there is this sad
entry for September 6, 1782: "My dear wife died this day
at 11 H. 45 A.M." That was all. A methodical man, Jefferson recorded the exact moment of her death. In May, just
four months before, Martha Wayles Jefferson had given
birth to her sixth child and Jefferson had made this hope-
ful entry on the leaf of his prayerbook, "Lucy Elizabeth
Jefferson, born May 8, 1782 at 1 o'clock A.M." Martha
never rallied from the ordeal, fading like a dying sunset
while her distracted husband hovered near her bedside,
watching, dreading, as her strength ebbed. She took leave
just as the first tints of autumn were streaking the foliage
on Jefferson's little mountain.

In the eighteenth century, child-bearing exacted a harsh

toll of both mother and offspring, and apparently Martha was even less successful than many others in creating life that could clear the hurdles of infancy. Of the six children she had borne Jefferson three were snuffed out quickly, including a son and heir whose arrival had gladdened his heart with high hopes only to be blighted within three weeks. In time he would lavish on a grandson the love he had stored up for a son of his own. Making entries in his prayerbook had become almost a habit with him.

Young, fragile, beautiful, Martha Jefferson was the love of Jefferson's life. She was twenty-three, he twenty-eight, when they married in 1772. No portrait of her is known to have been painted. At least none was ever found. Nothing remains but descriptions of her left by devoted friends —these and a secret drawer of mementos kept sacred from all eyes save those of her husband to the end of his days and an exquisite epitaph written by him and chiseled on a slab of now weathered marble in the burying ground on the eastern slope of his mountain.

Yet she would live on in the lives of the three little girls who survived her and to whom Jefferson must now be father and mother. There was her namesake, Martha, just turned ten, whom Jefferson endearingly called Patsy and sometimes Patty. She was to become the great comforter of his future sorrows, his intimate friend and companion. Her love and sympathy would solace the clouded evening of his life. Next came Mary, his Polly and often just plain Poll, who never remembered her mother, yet who, like her, would grow up frail and beautiful, only to die at the very peak of her father's career. With her going would fade much of the glory of being President of the United States. Lastly, there was tiny Lucy, four months old, for whom the mother had given her life. Lucy, too, would linger for a while, delicately, and then in a paroxysm of whooping cough, be snatched away while her father was minister plenipotentiary in Paris.

4

Jefferson never remarried. In her last moments—so the story goes and it seems not unlikely—Martha asked him never to marry again. His sorrow was so deep that seldom, if ever, in after years could he bring himself to speak her name. Nor is there in the vast array of his extant papers and letters barely more than a mention of her.

In 1782, Jefferson was already famous. As penman of the nation's birth certificate, his renown had spread across two continents. His political activities had brought him mounting honors. From his quill had flowed thousands of inspiring words during the build-up to revolution by the American colonies. From his brilliant service in the Continental Congress in 1776 he had returned to Virginia to fashion a new code of democratic laws for the now independent Commonwealth of Virginia and to become her second governor.

Meanwhile, he was building his architectural dream child. Leveling off the top of his 600-foot mountain, he crowned it with a classical, half-domed Palladian house to which he gave the felicitous Italian name, Monticello, destined to become one of the most fascinating homes in America. Its windows faced in every direction. Westward it looked away to the majestic barriers of the Blue Ridge Mountains. It was engirdled by a panorama of greenclad foothills and valleys. "Where," he once asked, "has Nature spread so rich a mantle? Mountains, forests, rocks and 2 rivers."

At thirty-eight Jefferson had retired from public life with dreams of becoming a rural philosopher perched on his mountain fastness far above the bickerings of politics. "I had folded myself in the arms of retirement and rested all my prospects of future happiness on domestic & literary objects." Glorifying it all would be the love of the beautiful woman he adored.

But these dreams were shattered that bitter day in September, 1782. "A single event wiped out all my plans and left me a blank which I had not the spirits to fill up." Just what the future held he knew not, nor cared. Yet, a practical man, he realized he faced a very pressing problem: he was the father of three orphaned girls, one just four months old, who needed his love and care.

Although the fires of grief died down, Monticello, the home he loved, seemed a dreary place without Martha, and for the only time in his life Jefferson felt that he would be glad to get away from it.

It was at this moment—three months after his wife's death—that the Confederation Congress offered him a place with the peace mission then in France negotiating the treaty with Great Britain that would end the American Revolution. This meant crossing the Atlantic to collaborate with ministers plenipotentiary Benjamin Franklin and John Adams in Paris. It also meant a return to the public life that he had eschewed. In his loneliness, however, he accepted the summons. A trip to Europe with new scenes and new duties would refresh him, stimulate him to new life. He would lose himself in work and service. It would give him an opportunity to see and taste the culture of France which he had always admired. But before posting his letter of acceptance, he must consider what to do about his children.

Reluctantly he decided to leave the little ones, Mary and Lucy, with their maternal aunt Mrs. Francis (Elizabeth) Eppes, who lived on a delightful plantation called Eppington on the Appomattox River below Richmond. The house—which little Mary would come to love even more than Monticello—was snowy white, with green shutters, a hipped roof, and two projecting wings with enough great-big rooms to shelter a dozen small folk. Best of all, kind and amiable Aunt Eppes had a brood of her own, Mary's five cousins, who rollicked about the house and spacious lawn. One of them, Jack Eppes, now nine, would one day lead Mary to the altar. Eppington was a child's paradise, with an abundant garden, always a new colt or calf to furnish excitement, and a dog or two lazying on the porch but ever ready to be played with. Here the two little Jeffersons found in Elizabeth Eppes the only mother they ever knew. She was the wife of Francis, Uncle Eppes, whom Jefferson once acclaimed as "the first horticulturist in America."

As for Martha, now ten, he would take her with him, and on a frosty day in December, 1782, leaving Monticello dark, closed, and chilly like the weather, he and the little girl climbed into his phaeton, drove down the mountain, and headed for Philadelphia where Congress was in session. In Philadelphia he placed Martha temporarily in a private school under the care of an estimable lady, Mrs. Thomas Hopkinson, mother of Francis Hopkinson, a co-signer with Jefferson and fifty-four others of the Declaration of Independence.

But the mission to France never got off the ground, or rather the ice. The French frigate *Romulus,* on which Jefferson was offered passage to France, lay locked in the ice below Baltimore. An added hazard was a British cruiser lurking off the Virginia capes to intercept the American envoy. Meanwhile, there was nothing to do but wait for a more propitious moment. Always one to put time to good use Jefferson set about informing himself "of the general state of our foreign relations" and recouping his old political finesse. Three months of waiting brought news from France that a provisional treaty of peace with Britain had been agreed on. Jefferson was released from his mission with the thanks of Congress for his "readiness in undertaking a service."

With Martha beside him he gloomily drove back to Virginia, reaching Monticello in mid-May, but joy had departed from his mountaintop eyrie. Although the hills and valleys were abloom, dogwood and redbud wearing robes of beauty, Jefferson saw them not. He was heartsick, a man of forty who had all but lost his bearings. While he groped aimlessly, his friends determined to lure him back into politics where his talents were much needed.

Early in June the Virginia Assembly appointed him a delegate to the Confederation Congress, and in October he and Martha again drove down the mountain and headed north for Philadelphia. There Jefferson restored Martha to the care of Mrs. Hopkinson, and hurried to catch up with Congress, then convened at Annapolis.

For the next six months Jefferson rendered yeoman service. Pressing problems faced the flimsy Confederation Congress: money, currency, foreign policy, public lands. Two of the state papers Jefferson laid before Congress became foundation stones of the Republic. He drew up the first plan of government for the Northwest Territory, the vast domain north of the Ohio and east of the Mississippi which Virginia had ceded to the Confederation. This plan provided the framework for the future expansion of the Union. He took a hand in establishing a money system for the new nation. From him came a classic paper suggesting the dollar as the basis of the nation's currency. Lastly he proposed that ministers be dispatched to all European nations to negotiate commercial treaties. As a guide to these ministers Jefferson drew up his celebrated "Instructions" for Americans representing the United States abroad.

On May 7, 1784, Congress again appointed Jefferson minister plenipotentiary, this time to collaborate in negotiating treaties of amity and commerce with European governments. His acceptance was immediate, he would join Franklin and Adams, who were still in Paris.

The earliest extant letters (to follow) from Thomas Jefferson to his beloved Patsy (Martha) are those written from Annapolis soon after taking his seat in the Confederation Congress in November, 1783. These were the first of hundreds he would write her during his lifetime. He wrote regularly, which is more than Martha apparently did. In later years he would chide her for not writing though always he tempered his words with those of affection.

If Jefferson's letters to his daughters sound preachy, if he seems to have lectured them, he always offered good counsel and oceans of affection. Determined that Martha should become an educated member of society, he gave the same scrupulous attention to her upbringing as to his duties in Congress or the greater tasks to which in time he would be summoned.

His first letter to Martha from Annapolis expressed his idea of what he considered the proper education for a lady of twelve. "The good lady under whose roof I have placed you" was Mrs. Hopkinson, of course. Mrs. Trist was a friend of Jefferson's whose grandson Nicholas Trist later married Jefferson's granddaughter Virginia Randolph. (This letter has an interesting sequel. In 1837 Princess Victoria of England, soon to become queen, requested the American chargé d'affaires at London to procure for her a letter of Thomas Jefferson's for her autograph collection. In due time Jefferson's grandson, Thomas Jefferson Randolph, dispatched this letter to the princess who returned her royal thanks. Presumably, the letter is still in the possession of Britain's ruling family.)

My Dear Patsy   Annapolis, Nov. 28, 1783
After four days journey I arrived here without any accident and in as good health as when I left Philadelphia. The conviction that you would be more improved in the situation I have placed you than if still with me, has solaced me on my parting with you, which my love for you has rendered a difficult thing. The acquirements which I hope you will make under the tutors I have provided for you will render you more worthy of my love, and if they cannot increase it they will prevent it's diminution. Consider the good lady who has taken you under her roof, who has undertaken to see that

you perform all your exercises, and to admonish you in all those wanderings from what is right or what is clever to which your inexperience would expose you, consider her I say as your mother, as the only person to whom, since the loss with which heaven has been pleased to afflict you, you can now look up; and that her displeasure or disapprobation on any occasion will be an immense misfortune which should you be so unhappy as to incur by any unguarded act, think no concession too much to regain her good will. With respect to the distribution of your time the following is what I should approve.

from 8. to 10 o'clock practise music.

from 10. to 1. dance one day and draw another.

from 1. to 2. draw on the day you dance, and write a letter the next day.

from 3. to 4. read French.

from 4. to 5. exercise yourself in music.

from 5. till bedtime read English, write etc.

Communicate this plan to Mrs. Hopkinson and if she approves of it pursue it. As long as Mrs. Trist remains in Philadelphia cultivate her affections. She has been a valuable friend to you and her good sense and good heart make her valued by all who know her and by nobody on earth more than by me. I expect you will write to me by every post. Inform me what books you read, what tunes you learn, and inclose me your best copy of every lesson in drawing. Write also one letter every week either to your aunt Eppes, your aunt Skipwith, your aunt Carr, or the little lady from whom I now inclose a letter, and always put the letter you so write under cover to me. Take care that you never spell a word wrong. Always before you write a word consider how it is spelt, and if you do not remember it, turn to a dictionary. It produces great praise to a lady to spell well. I have placed my happiness on seeing you good and accomplished, and no distress which this world can now bring on me could equal that of your disappointing my hopes. If you love me then, strive to be good under every situation and to all living creatures, and to acquire those accomplishments which I have put in your power, and which will go far towards ensuring you the warmest love of your affectionate father,

Th: Jefferson

P.S. keep my letters and read them at times that you may always have present in your mind those things which will endear you to me.

> Martha's reply to this letter has never been found. Although Jefferson's journal of letters received lists several from Patsy during these months, none has ever turned up. But apparently she had been disturbed by someone's prediction that the end of the world was at hand and had written asking her father what to do about it. His reply sought to calm her fears. (The "Mr. Cimitiere"—or "Cimetiere" or "Simitiere," as Jefferson variously spelled it— mentioned in the next letter was DuSimitière, an eminent Frenchman residing in Philadelphia, who painted miniatures and taught drawing.)

My Dear Patsy   Annapolis Dec. 11. 1783

I wrote you by the post this day fortnight, since which I have received two letters from you. I am afraid that you may not have sent to the post office and therefore that my letter may be still lying there. Tho' my business here may not let me write to you every week yet it will not be amiss for you to enquire at the office every week. I wrote to Mr. House by the last post. Perhaps his letter may still be in the office. I hope you will have good sense enough to disregard those foolish predictions that the world is to be at an end soon. The almighty has never made known to any body at what time he created it, nor will he tell any body when he means to put an end to it, if ever he means to do it. As to preparations for that event, the best way is for you to be always prepared for it. The only way to be so is never to do nor say a bad thing. If ever you are about to say any thing amiss or to do any thing wrong, consider before hand. You will feel something within you which will tell you it is wrong and ought not to be said or done: this is your conscience, and be sure to obey it. Our maker has given us all, this faithful internal Monitor, and if you always obey it, you will always be prepared for the end of the world: or for a much more certain event which is death. This must happen to all: it puts an end to the world as to us, and the way to be ready for it is never to do a wrong act. I am glad you are proceeding regularly under your tutors. You must not let the sickness of your French master interrupt your reading French, because you are able to do that with the help of your dictionary. Remember I desired you to send me the best copy you should make of every lesson Mr. Cimitiere should set you. In this I hope you will be punctual, because it will let me see how you are going on. Always let me know too what tunes you play. Present my compliments to Mrs. Hopkinson, Mrs. House and Mrs. Trist. I had a letter from your uncle Eppes last week informing me that Polly is very well, and Lucy recovered from an indisposition. I am my dear Patsy Your affectionate father,

Th: Jefferson

The day Jefferson wrote this next letter—December 22, 1783—Annapolis was in a gala mood. A historic event was in the offing. On the morrow, in a moving, dramatic scene, George Washington would appear before Congress to resign his commission as commander in chief of the Revolutionary armies. His sword sheathed, his country free, he would retire to private life. To Jefferson's pen has always been ascribed the beautiful response of the President of

Congress to Washington's address of resignation. Apparently Jefferson composed it the day he wrote this letter to Martha. Yet not a word of the historic scenes unfolding around him appears in this letter in which he admonishes Martha on untidiness in dress. He had asked a friend in Philadelphia to find out how she was getting along in school. The friend had replied she was doing well in her studies though apparently she was a bit careless in her dress. This report brought Jefferson's admonishing letter, now in the Library of Congress.

My Dear Patsy   Annapolis Dec. 22. 1783
I hoped before this to have received letters from you regularly and weekly by the post, and also to have had a letter to forward from you to one of your aunts as I desired in my letter of November 27th. I am afraid you do not comply with my desires expressed in that letter. Your not writing to me every week is one instance, and your having never sent me any of your copies of Mr. Simitiere's lessons is another. I shall be very much mortified and disappointed if you become inattentive to my wishes and particularly to the directions of that letter which I meant for your principal guide. I omitted in that to advise you on the subject of dress, which I know you are a little apt to neglect. I do not wish you to be gayly clothed at this time of life, but that what you wear should be fine of it's kind; but above all things, & at all times let your clothes be clean, whole, and properly put on. do not fancy you must wear them till the dirt is visible to the eye. You will be the last who will be sensible of this. some ladies think they may under the privileges of the dishabille be loose & negligent of their dress in the morning. but be you from the moment you rise till you go to bed as cleanly and properly dressed as at the hours of dinner or tea. A lady who has been seen as a sloven or slut in the morning, will never efface the

impression she then made with all the dress and pageantry she can afterwards involve herself in. nothing is so disgusting to our sex as a want of cleanliness and delicacy in yours. I hope therefore the moment you rise from bed, your first work will be to dress yourself in such a stile as that you may be seen by any gentleman without his being able to discover a pin amiss, or any other circumstance of neatness wanting.

By a letter from Mr. Short [Jefferson's secretary] I learn that your sisters are well. I hope I shall soon receive a letter from you informing me you are so. I wrote a letter to Polly lately, which I supposed her aunt would read to her. I dare say it pleased her, as would a letter from you. I am sorry Mrs. Trist has determined to go at so inclement a season, as I fear she will suffer much more than she expects. present my compliments to her and the good family there, as also very particularly to Mrs. Hopkinson whose health and happiness I have much at heart. I hope you are obedient & respectful to her in every circumstance and that your manners will be such as to engage her affections. I am my dear Patsy Yours sincerely & affectionately,

Th: Jefferson

> The "worthy family" whom Jefferson offers for Martha's admiration was that of the mechanical genius, clockmaker, and gifted astronomer David Rittenhouse, to whom Jefferson reported his observations on the eclipse of 1778.

My Dear Patsy   Annapolis Jan. 15. 1784.
Your letter by the post is not yet come to hand, that by Mr. Beresford I received this morning. Your long silence had induced me almost to suspect you had forgotten me and the more so as I had desired you to write to me every week. I am anxious to know what books you read, what tunes you can

play, and to receive specimens of your drawings. With respect to your meeting Mr. Simitiere at Mr. Rittenhouse's, nothing could give me more pleasure than your being much with that worthy family wherein you will see the best examples of rational life and learn to esteem and copy them. But I should be very tender of obtruding you on the family as it might perhaps be not always convenient to them for you to be there at your hours of attending Mr. Simitiere. I can only say then that if it has been desired by Mr. and Mrs. Rittenhouse in such a way as that Mrs. Hopkinson shall be satisfied they will not consider it as inconvenient, I would have you thankfully accept it and conduct yourself with so much attention to the family as that they may never feel themselves incommoded by it. I hope Mrs. Hopkinson will be so good as to act for you in this matter with that delicacy and prudence of which she is so capable. I have so much at heart your learning to draw, and should be uneasy at your losing this opportunity which probably is your last. But I remind you to inclose me every week a copy of all your lessons in drawing that I may judge how you come on. I have had very ill health since I came here. I have been just able to attend my duty in the state house, but not to go out on any other occasion. I am however considerably better. Present my highest esteem to Mrs. Hopkinson and accept yourself assurances of the sincere love with which I am my dear Patsy, Yours affectionately,

Th: Jefferson

Dear Patsy   Annapolis Feb. 18. 1784.
I have received two or three letters from you since I wrote last. Indeed my health has been so bad that I have been able scarcely to read, write or do any thing else. Your letters to your aunt and the others shall be forwarded. I hope you will continue to inclose to me every week one for some of

your friends in Virginia. I am sorry Mr. Cimetiere cannot attend you, because it is probable you will never have another opportunity of learning to draw, and it is a pretty and pleasing accomplishment. With respect to the paiment of the guinea, I would wish him to receive it, because if there is to be a doubt between him and me, which of us acts rightly, I would chuse to remove it clearly off my own shoulders. You must thank Mrs. Hopkinson for me for the trouble she gave herself in this matter, from which she will be relieved by paying Mr. Cimetiere his demand. Perhaps when the season becomes milder he will consent to attend you. I am sorry your French master cannot be more punctual. I hope you nevertheless read French every day as I advised you. Your letter to me in French gave me great satisfaction and I wish you to exercise yourself in the same way frequently. Your sisters are well. I am in hopes the money I had placed in the bank subject to Mrs. Hopkinson's order had not yet failed. Lest it should have done so, inform her that I have now sent there a further supply. Deliver my most respectful compliments to her & be assured of the love with which I am My dear Patsy Your's affectionately,

Th: Jefferson

Dear Patsy   Annapolis Mar. 19. 1784.
It is now very long since I have had a letter from you. I hope you continue in good health, and attention to the several objects for which I placed you in Philadelphia. I take for granted you go on with your music and dancing, that when your French master can attend, you receive his instructions, and read by yourself when he cannot. Let me know what books you have read since I left you, and what tunes you can play. Have you been able to coax Cimetiere to continue? Letters by yesterday's post inform me your sisters are well. I inclose you a letter I received from Dear Polly. I send here-

with Mr. Zane's present of the looking glass which I dare say he intended for you. Wait upon Mrs. House and let her know, if she should not have heard from Mrs. Trist lately, that we have received a letter from her by a gentleman immediately from Fort Pitt. She is very well and expects to leave that place about the first of April. Present me in the most friendly terms to your patroness Mrs. Hopkinson & be assured of the love with which I am Dr. Patsy Yours affectionately,

Th: Jefferson

Mr. Maury will deliver you this, who is lately from Virginia and is my particular friend.

My Dear Patsy   Annapolis Apr. 4. 1784. This will be handed you by Genl. Gates, who going to Philadelphia furnishes me with the opportunity of writing to you. I am again getting my health, and have some expectations of going to Philadelphia ere long; but of this am not certain. I have had no letters from Eppington since I wrote you last, and have not received one from you I think these two months. I wish to know what you read, what tunes you play, how you come on in your writing, whether you have been able to persuade Simetiere to continue, how you do, and how Mrs. Hopkinson does. These are articles of intelligence which will always be pleasing to me. Present my compliments respectfully to Mrs. Hopkinson, give her occasion always to be pleased with your grateful returns for the kind care she takes of you, and be assured of the love with which I am Dr. Patsy Yours affectionately,

Th: Jefferson

My Dear Patsy   Annapolis Apr. 17. 1784. I have not received a letter from you since early in February. This is far short of my injunctions to write once a week by

immediately for the stay maker, the mantua makers, the milliner and even a shoemaker before I could go out. I never had the *friseur* but once, but I soon got rid of him and turned down my hair in spite of all they could say, and I defer it now as much as possible for I think it always too soon to suffer.

After a month of sightseeing Jefferson resolved his next problem: finding a suitable school for Martha. Through the good offices of Lafayette he entered her in the Abbaye Royale de Panthemont convent school, the most fashionable and expensive in France. Here young ladies were finished off in the arts, in music, languages, etiquette, and dancing—also in wearing a crimson uniform "made like a frock laced behind, with the tail like a *robe de cour*, hooked on, muslin cuffs and tuckers."

On August 30, 1784, the American ministers plenipotentiary held their first meeting at Dr. Franklin's home in Passy outside of Paris. Their task was to implement the peace treaty with Great Britain by one of amity and trade. They were further empowered to make treaty advances to sixteen European nations and the Barbary States. Not too much came of their first efforts.

In 1785, Benjamin Franklin, full of years and honors, retired as minister plenipotentiary to the Court of Versailles. The grand old statesman and philosopher had long yearned to return to his native heath "to lay his bones down." Congress quickly appointed Jefferson to succeed him. It was not easy for Jefferson to assume the mantle of Franklin whose wit, wisdom, and *bonhomie* had endeared him to all France. But in time Jefferson would occupy as conspicuous a place perhaps in French hearts as had his predecessor. In his first official contact with Count de Vergennes, the celebrated French minister of foreign affairs, Jefferson tossed off a bon mot that caught the ear of every Frenchman. "I hear you come to replace Monsieur Franklin," observed the count. "No," replied Jefferson, "I only succeed him. No one can replace him."

In 1786, Jefferson crossed the English Channel for a two months' visit to the kingdom whose sovereign he had belabored so resoundingly in the Declaration of Independence. John Adams was now American minister plenipotentiary to Great Britain. The object of Jefferson's visit was to team up with Adams in negotiating a treaty with the piratical Barbary States whose minister in London had approached Adams on the subject. Jefferson and Adams got nowhere with the "Barbarian minister,"' but they had an enthralling round of sightseeing through many of the famous English residences and gardens Jefferson had read about but never dreamed of seeing.

On the day of his departure from Paris, he wrote Martha a good-by letter.

My dear Martha: Paris Mar. 6. 1786
I shall be absent so short a time that any letter you would write me would hardly get to London before I should be coming away; and it is the more discouraging as they open all letters in the post office. Should however sickness or any other circumstance render a letter to me necessary, send it here to Mr. Short and he will direct and forward it. I shall defer engaging your drawing master till I return. I hope then to find you most advanced in your music. I need not tell you what pleasure it gives me to see you improve in everything agreeable and useful. The more you learn the more I love you, and I rest the happiness of my life on seeing you beloved by all the world, which you will be sure to be if to a good heart you join those accomplishments so peculiarly pleasing in your sex. Adieu my dear child; lose no moment in improving your head, nor any opportunity of exercising your heart in benevolence. Yours affectionately,

Th: Jefferson

By 1787, Jefferson was a conspicuous, much-sought-after figure in Paris. His "Dear Patsy" was now fifteen, warm, affectionate, intelligent. Tall like her father, but, like him, no beauty, yet most attractive. Three years at the Panthemont school had made her a polished young lady. She danced well. She caught on to the language even better than her father. He said so himself. She had acquired many of the graces necessary to a young lady and particularly to the daughter of the American minister plenipotentiary to the Court of Louis XVI and Marie Antoinette. She had even been taught how to behave when presented to the King and Queen, a ceremony she found almost as amusing as did her father.

On a rainy day in February, 1787, Jefferson climbed into his carriage, turned his horse's head south, and drove out of Paris for his first vacation since he had landed in France. He traveled alone in his own glass-doored and windowed equipage. He visited Martha at the Panthemont before he left. To keep her from being lonely in his absence he planned to write her long letters describing what he saw and the wonderful places he visited. In turn she promised to write him regularly. He drew for her an elaborate road map showing just where he would be, and when, so that he could be sure of receiving her letters.

On this carefree journey to southern France and northern Italy, Jefferson would realize his long-cherished dream of seeing a world he had hoped to see all his life. He would gaze on the sparkling blue waters of the Mediterranean, drink in the glory of the Alps, feast on the wonders of Roman antiquity and the remains of its civilization.

Jogging along easily, his observant eye took in everything: "the culture and the cultivated," how the people lived, how they were clothed, what they ate, their relaxation, their poverty. He walked across their olive fields and orangeries. He inspected their vineyards and winemaking. He poked into hovels, castles, and palaces. He filled his notebook with more than twenty thousand words on things he saw that could be useful in America. To his secretary, William Short, he wrote from Lyon, "Architecture, painting, sculpture, agriculture and the condition of the poor fill all my moments."

At Nîmes he lost his heart to the remains of a Roman temple, the Maison Carrée (Square House). So smitten was he by its beauty that he indited a love letter to this monument of Roman grandeur, though addressing it to his old friend Madam de Tessé: "Here I am, Madame, gazing whole hours at the Maison Carrée, like a lover at his mistress."

On March 29, 1787, Jefferson reached Aix-en-Provence. Ostensibly he went there to drink the healing waters of Aix for his dislocated wrist that refused to mend. He stayed just long enough to "prove the inefficacy of the waters." At Aix, Martha's first letter caught up with him. She was having difficulty translating the commentaries of Titus Livius (Livy). Apparently Latin was her chief stumbling block. She was relying on her "master." As for Livy, she said, he "puts me out of my wits."

Panthemont february (March?) 8 1787 being disappointed in my expectation of receiving a letter from my dear papa, I have resolved to break so painful a silence by giving you an example that I hope you will follow, particularly as you know how much pleasure your letters give me. I hope your wrist is better and I am inclined to think that your voyage is rather for your pleasure than for your health. however I hope it will answer both purposes. I will now tell you how I go on with my masters. I have begun a beautiful tune with balbastre, done a very pretty landskip with Pariseau a little man playing on the violin and began another beautiful landskape. I go on very slowly with my *tite live* its being in such ancient italian that I can not

read with out my master and very little with him even. as for
the dansing master I intend to leave him off as soon as my
month is finished tell me if you are still determined that I
shall dine at the abesse's table. if you are I shall at the end of
my quarter. the kings speach and that of the eveque de nar-
bone has been copied all over the convent. as for Monseur he
rose up to speak but sat down again with out daring to open
his lips. I have no news but supose Mr. Short will write you
enough for him and me too. Mde. Thaubenen desires her
compliments to you adieu my dear papa I am afraid you
will not be able to read my scrawl, but I have not the time
of coppying it over again. therefore I must beg your indulgence and assure [you] of the tender affections of yours,

M. Jefferson
pray write often and long letters.

March 25th, 1787
My dear Papa—Though the knowledge of your health gave
me the greatest pleasure, yet I own I was not a little disappointed in not receiving a letter from you. However, I console myself with the thought of having one very soon, as you
promised to write me every week. Until now you have not
kept your word the least in the world, but I hope you will
make up for your silence by writing me a fine, long letter
by the first opportunity. *Titus Livius* puts me out of my wits.
I can not read a word by myself, and I read of it very seldom with my master; however, I hope I shall soon be able to
take it up again. All my other masters go on much the same
—perhaps better. Every body here is very well, particularly
Madame L'Abbesse, who has visited almost a quarter of the
new building—a thing that she has not done for two or three
years before now. I have not heard any thing of my harpsichord, and I am afraid it will not come before your arrival.
They make every day some new history on the Assemblee des

being disapointed in my expectation of receiving a
letter from my dear papa I have resolved to break so
painful a silence by giving you an example that
I hope you will follow particularly as you know how
much pleasure your letters give me I hope your wrist
is better and I am inclined to think that your voyage
is rather for your pleasure than for your health
however I hope it will answer both purposes. I will
now tell you how I go on with my masters I have began
a beautiful tune with balbastre done a very pretty
landship with Pariseau a little man playing on the
violin and began another beautiful landskape I go on
very slowly with my tite live its being in such ancient
italian that I can nott read with out my master
and very little with him even. as for the dancing
master I intend to leave him off as soon as my month
is finished tell me if you are still determined that

*While Jefferson was minister to France, Martha Jefferson attended the
Panthemont school in Paris. Although she was an outstanding student,
she was having trouble—as she writes her father on February 6, 1787—
with the difficult Latin of Titus Livius' history of the Roman people.
(Courtesy of the Massachusetts Historical Society.)*

Notables. I will not tell you any, for fear of taking a trip to the Bastile for my pains, which I am by no means disposed to do at this moment. I go on pretty well with Thucydides, and hope I shall very soon finish it. I expect Mr. Short every instant for my letter, therefore I must leave you. Adieu, my dear papa; be assured you are never a moment absent from my thoughts, and believe me to be, your most affectionate child,

M. Jefferson.

Jefferson's reply contained much of his philosophy of life, pointing out the virtue of industry. To this letter he committed his panegyric on the "American character." He feared she was taking the world too easily. She must not lean too heavily on her "master" in translating Latin; she must be more self-reliant. But he sealed his letter with love.

Aix-en-Provence, March 28th, 1787

I was happy, my dear Patsy, to receive, on my arrival here, your letter, informing me of your good health and occupation. I have not written to you sooner because I have been almost constantly on the road. My journey hitherto has been a very pleasing one. It was undertaken with the hope that the mineral-waters of this place might restore strength to my wrist. Other considerations also concurred—instruction, amusement, and abstraction from business, of which I had too much at Paris. I am glad to learn that you are employed in things new and good, in your music and drawing. You know what have been my fears for some time past—that you do not employ yourself so closely as I could wish. You have promised me a more assiduous attention, and I have great confidence in what you promise. It is your future happiness which interests me, and nothing can contribute more to it (moral rectitude always excepted) than the contracting a habit of industry and activity. Of all the cankers of human happiness none corrodes with so silent, yet so baneful an influence, as indolence. Body and mind both unemployed, our being becomes a burthen, and every object about us loathsome, even the dearest. Idleness begets ennui, ennui the hypochondriac, and that a diseased body. No laborious person was ever yet hysterical. Exercise and application produce order in our affairs, health of body and cheerfulness of mind, and these make us precious to our friends. It is while we are young that the habit of industry is formed. If not then, it never is afterwards. The fortune of our lives, therefore, depends on employing well the short period of youth. If at any moment, my dear, you catch yourself in idleness, start from it as you would from the precipice of a gulf. You are not, however, to consider yourself as unemployed, while taking exercise. That is necessary for your health, and health is the first of all objects. For this reason, if you leave your dancing-master for the summer, you must increase your other exercise.

I do not like your saying that you are unable to read the ancient print of your Livy but with the aid of your master. We are always equal to what we undertake with resolution. A little degree of this will enable you to decipher your Livy. If you always lean on your master, you will never be able to proceed without him. It is a part of the American character to consider nothing as desperate; to surmount every difficulty by resolution and contrivance. In Europe there are shops for every want; its inhabitants, therefore, have no idea that their wants can be supplied otherwise. Remote from all other aid, we are obliged to invent and to execute; to find means within ourselves, and not to lean on others. Consider, therefore, the conquering your Livy as an exercise in the habit of surmounting difficulties; a habit which will be necessary to you in the country where you are to live, and without which you will be thought a very helpless animal, and less esteemed. Music, drawing, books, invention, and exercise, will be so many resources to you against ennui. But there are others which, to this object, add that of utility. These are the needle and domestic economy. The latter you can not learn here, but the former you may. In the country life of America there are many moments when a woman can have recourse to nothing but her needle for employment. In a dull company, and in dull weather, for instance, it is ill-manners to read, it is ill-manners to leave them; no card-playing there among genteel people—that is abandoned to blackguards. The needle is then a valuable resource. Besides, without knowing how to use it herself, how can the mistress of a family direct the work of her servants?

You ask me to write you long letters. I will do it, my dear, on condition you will read them from time to time, and practice what they inculcate. Their precepts will be dictated by experience, by a perfect knowledge of the situation in which you will be placed, and by the fondest love for you. This it is which makes me wish to see you more qualified than common. My expectations from you are high, yet not higher than you may attain. Industry and resolution are all that are wanting. Nobody in this world can make me so happy, or so miserable, as you. Retirement from public life will ere long become necessary for me. To your sister and yourself I look to render the evening of my life serene and contented. Its morning has been clouded by loss after loss, till I have nothing left but you. I do not doubt either your affections or dispositions. But great exertions are necessary, and you have little time left to make them. Be industrious, then, my dear child. think nothing insurmountable by resolution and application, and you will be all that I wish you to be.

You ask if it is my desire that you should dine at the Abbess's table? It is. Propose it as such to Madame de Traubenheim, with my respectful compliments, and thanks for her care of you. Continue to love me with all the warmth with which you are beloved by, my dear Patsy,

Yours affectionately,

Th. Jefferson.

Jefferson's next letter to Martha, written from Toulon, has often been hailed as a model of letter-writing style. There is a further side to this letter. Jefferson's little Mary, now nine, whom he had left with his sister-in-law, Mrs. Francis Eppes, at Eppington, in Virginia, was on her way across the Atlantic to join her father and sister. She might arrive any day. Actually, Mary arrived about four months after the date of this letter.

My Dear Patsy   Toulon April 7. 1787
I received yesterday at Marseilles your letter of March 25. and I received it with pleasure because it announced to me that you were well. experience learns us to be always anxious about the health of those whom we love. I have not been able to write to you so often as I expected, because I am generally on the road; & when I stop any where, I am occupied in seeing what is to be seen. it will be some time now, perhaps three weeks before I shall be able to write to you again. but this need not slacken your writing to me, because you have leisure, & your letters come regularly to me. I have received letters which inform me that our dear Polly will certainly come to us this summer. by the time I return it will be time to expect her. When she arrives, she will become a precious charge on your hands. the difference of your age, and your common loss of a mother, will put that office on you. teach her above all things to be good: because without that we

My dear Patsy   Toulon April 7 1787.

I received yesterday at Marseilles your letter of March
25. and I received it with pleasure because it announced to
me that you were well. experience learns us to be always
anxious about the health of those whom we love. I have not been
able to write to you so often as I expected, because I am generally
on the road; & when I stop any where, I am occupied in seeing what
is to be seen. it will be some time now, perhaps three weeks be-
-fore I shall be able to write to you again. but this need not
slacken your writing to me, because you have leisure, & your
letters come regularly to me. I have received letters which inform me that our dear Polly will certainly come to us this
summer. by the time I return it will be time to expect her.
when she arrives, she will become a precious charge on your
hands. the difference of your age, and your common loss of a
mother, will put that office on you. teach her above all things
to be good: because without that we can neither be valued by
others, nor set any value on ourselves. teach her to be always
true. no vice is so mean as the want of truth, & at the same
time so useless. teach her never to be angry. anger only serves
to torment ourselves, to divert others, and alienate their es-
-teem. and teach her industry & application to useful pursuits.

I will venture to assure you that if you inculcate this in her mind you will make her a happy being in herself, a most inestimable friend to you, and precious to all the world. in teaching her these dispositions of mind, you will be more fixed in them yourself, and render yourself dear to all your acquaintance. practice them then, my dear, without ceasing. if ever you find yourself in difficulty and doubt ~~how~~ how to extricate, yourself, do what is right, & you will find it the easiest way of getting out of the difficulty. do it for the additional incitement of increasing the happiness of him who loves you infinitely, and who is my dear Patsy

yours affectionately

Th. Jefferson

April 7. ..87

In this letter to "Dear Patsy" (April 7, 1787) Jefferson looks forward hopefully to the coming of Maria, when the tiny family would once again be reunited. It was written from Toulon, which Jefferson visited on his journey through southern France in 1787. (Courtesy of the J. Pierpont Morgan Library, New York City.)

can neither be valued by others, nor set any value on ourselves. teach her to be always true. no vice is so mean as the
want of truth, & at the same time so useless. teach her never
to be angry. anger only serves to torment ourselves, to divert
others, and alienate their esteem. and teach her industry &
application to useful pursuits. I will venture to assure you
that if you inculcate this in her mind you will make her a
happy being in herself, a most inestimable friend to you,
and precious to all the world. in teaching her these dispositions of mind, you will be more fixed in them yourself, and
render yourself dear to all your acquaintances. practice them
then, my dear, without ceasing. if ever you find yourself in
difficulty and doubt how to extricate yourself, do what is
right, & you will find it the easiest way of getting out of the
difficulty. do it for the additional incitement of increasing
the happiness of him who loves you infinitely, and who is
my dear Patsy your's affectionately,

Th. Jefferson

Panthemont, April 9th, 1787
My dear Papa—I am very glad that the beginning of your
voyage has been so pleasing, and I hope that the rest will be
not less so, as it is a great consolation for me, being deprived
of the pleasure of seeing you, to know at least that you are
happy. I hope your resolution of returning in the end of
April is always the same. I do not doubt but what Mr. Short
has written you word that my sister sets off with Fulwar
Skipwith in the month of May, and she will be here in July.
Then, indeed, shall I be the happiest of mortals; united to
what I have the dearest in the world, nothing more will be
requisite to render my happiness complete. I am not so industrious as you or I would wish, but I hope that in taking
pains I very soon shall be. I have already begun to study
more. I have not heard any news of my harpsichord; it will

be really very disagreeable if it is not here before your arrival. I am learning a very pretty thing now, but it is very hard. I .have drawn several little flowers, all alone, that the master even has not seen; indeed, he advised me to draw as much alone as possible for that is of more use than all I could do with him. I shall take up my Livy, as you desire it. I shall begin it again, as I have lost the thread of the history. As for the hysterics, you may be quiet on that head, as I am not lazy enough to fear them. Mrs. Barett has wanted me out, but Mr. Short told her that you had forgotten to tell Madame L'Abbesse to let me to go out with her. There was a gentleman, a few days ago, that killed himself because he thought that his wife did not love him. They had been married ten years. I believe that if every husband in Paris was to do as much, there would be nothing but widows left. I shall speak to Madame Thaubeneu about dining at the Abbess's table. As for needlework, the only kind that I could learn here would be embroidery, indeed netting also; but I could not do much of those in America, because of the impossibility of having proper silks; however, they will not be totally useless. You say your expectations for me are high, yet not higher than I can attain. Then be assured, my dear papa, that you shall be satisfied in that, as well as in any thing else that lies in my power; for what I hold most precious is your satisfaction, indeed I should be miserable without it. You wrote me a long letter, as I asked you; however, it would have been much more so without so wide a margin. Adieu, my dear papa. Be assured of the tenderest affection of your loving daughter,

M. Jefferson

Pray answer me very soon—a long letter, without a margin. I will try to follow the advice they contain with the most scrupulous exactitude.

My Dear Papa   Paris May 3 1787

I was very sorry to see by your letter to Mr. Short that your return would be put off, however I hope of not much, as you must be here for the arival of my sister. I wish I was my self all that you tell me to make her, however I will try to be as near like it as I can. I have another landskape since I wrote to you last and began another peice of music. I have not been able to do more having been confined some time to my bed with a violent head ake and a pain in my side which afterwards blistered up and made me suffer a great deal. But I am now much better. I have seen a phisician who has just drawn two of my companions out of a most dreadful situation which gave me a great deal of trust in him but the most disagreable is that I have been obliged to discontinue all my masters and am able now to take only some of them, those that are the least fatiguing. However I hope soon to take them all very soon. Mde. L'abesse has just had a fluxion de poitrine and has been at the last extremity but now is better. The *pays bas* have revolted against the emperor who is gone to Prussia to join with the empress and the venitians to war against the turcs. The plague is in spain. A virginia ship comming to spain met with a corser [corsair] of the same strength. They fought And the battle lasted an hour and a quarter. The Americans gained and boarded the corser where they found chains that had been prepared for them. They took them and made use of them for the algerians themselves. They returned to virginia from whence they are to go back to algers to change the prisoners to which if the algerians will not consent the poor creatures will be sold as slaves. Good god have we not enough? I wish with all my soul that the poor negroes were all freed. It greives my heart when I think that these our fellow creatures should be treated so teribly as they are by many of our country men. A coach and six well shut up was seen to go to the bastille and the baron de Breteuil went two hours before to prepare an apartment. They supose it to be Mde. De Polignac and her sister, however no one knows. The king asked M. D'harcourt how much a year was necessary for the Duphin. M. D'harcourt [after] having looked over the accounts told [him] two millions upon which the king could [not] help expressing his astonishment because each of his daughters cost him nine, so Mde. de Polignac has pocketed the rest. Mr. Smith is at Paris. That is all the news I know. They told me a great deal more but I have forgot it. Adieu my dear papa believe me to be for life your most tender and affectionate child,

M Jefferson

Marseilles, May 5th, 1787

My dear Patsy—I got back to Aix the day before yesterday, and found there your letter of the 9th of April—from which I presume you to be well, though you do not say so. In order to exercise your geography, I will give you a detail of my journey. You must therefore take your map and trace out the following places: Dijon, Lyons, Pont St. Esprit, Nismes, Arles, St. Remis, Aix, Marseilles, Toulon, Hieres, Frejus, Antibes, Nice, Col de tende, Coni, Turin, Vercelli, Milan, Pavia, Tortona, Novi, Genoa, by sea to Albenga, by land to Monaco, Nice, Antibes, Frejus, Brignolles, Aix, and Marseilles. The day after tomorrow, I set out hence for Aix, Avignon, Pont du Gard, Nismes, Montpellier, Narbonne, along the Canal of Languedoc to Toulouse, Bordeaux, Rochefort, Rochelle, Nantes, L'Orient, Nantes, Tours, Orleans, and Paris—where I shall arrive about the middle of June, after having travelled something upwards of a thousand leagues.

From Genoa to Aix was very fatiguing—the first two days having been at sea, and mortally sick—two more clambering the cliffs of the Apennines, sometimes on foot, sometimes on a mule, according as the path was more or less difficult—and two others travelling through the night as well as day without sleep. I am not yet rested, and shall therefore shortly give you rest by closing my letter, after mentioning that I have received a letter from your sister, which, though a year old, gave me great pleasure. I inclose it for your perusal, as I think it will be pleasing for you also. But take care of it, and return it to me when I shall get back to Paris, for, trifling as it seems, it is precious to me.

When I left Paris, I wrote to London to desire that your harpsichord might be sent during the months of April and May, so that I am in hopes it will arrive a little before I shall, and give me an opportunity of judging whether you have got the better of that want of industry which I began to fear would be the rock on which you would split.

Determine never to be idle. No person will have occasion to complain of the want of time who never loses any. It is wonderful how much may be done if we are always doing. And that you may be always doing good, my dear, is the ardent prayer of, yours affectionately,

Th. Jefferson

May 21st, 1787.

I write you, my dear Patsy, from the canal of Languedoc, on which I am at present sailing, as I have been for a week past, cloudless skies above, limpid waters below, and on each hand, a row of nightingales in full chorus. This delightful bird had given me a rich treat before, at the fountain of Vaucluse. After visiting the tomb of Laura at Avignon, I went to see this fountain—a noble one of itself, and rendered famous forever by the songs of Petrarch, who lived near it. I arrived there somewhat fatigued, and sat down by the fountain to repose myself. It gushes, of the size of a river, from a

secluded valley of the mountain, the ruins of Petrarch's cha-
teau being perched on a rock two hundred feet perpendicu-
lar above. To add to the enchantment of the scene, every
tree and bush was filled with nightingales in full song. I
think you told me that you had not yet noticed this bird.
As you have trees in the garden of the convent, there might
be nightingales in them, and this is the season of their song.
Endeavor, my dear, to make yourself acquainted with the
music of this bird, that when you return to your own country
you may be able to estimate its merit in comparison with
that of the mocking-bird. The latter has the advantage of
singing through a great part of the year, whereas the night-
ingale sings but about five or six weeks in the spring, and a
still shorter term, and with a more feeble voice, in the fall.

I expect to be at Paris about the middle of next month.
By that time we may begin to expect our dear Polly. It will
be a circumstance of inexpressible comfort to me to have
you both with me once more. The object most interesting
to me for the residue of my life, will be to see you both
developing daily those principles of virtue and goodness
which will make you valuable to others and happy in your-
selves, and acquiring those talents and that degree of science
which will guard you at all times against ennui, the most
dangerous poison of life. A mind always employed is always
happy. This is the true secret, the grand recipe, for felicity.
The idle are the only wretched. In a world which furnishes
so many employments which are useful, so many which are
amusing, it is our own fault if we ever know what ennui is, or
if we are ever driven to the miserable resource of gaming,
which corrupts our dispositions, and teaches us a habit of
hostility against all mankind. We are now entering the port
of Toulouse, where I quit my bark, and of course must conclude my letter. Be good and be industrious, and you will be

what I shall most love in the world. Adieu, my dear child. Yours affectionately,

Th. Jefferson.

Paris, May 27, 1787.

My dear Papa—I was very glad to see by your letter that you were on your return, and I hope that I shall very soon have the pleasure of seeing you. My sister's letter gave me a great deal of happiness. I wish she would write to me; but as I shall enjoy her presence very soon, it will make up for a neglect that I own gives me the greatest pain. I still remember enough of geography to know where the places marked in your letter are. I intend to copy over my extracts and learn them by heart. I have learnt several new pieces on the harpsichord, drawn five landscapes and three flowers, and hope to have done something more by the time you come. I go on pretty well with my history, and as for *Tite Live* I have begun it three or four times, and go on so slowly with it that I believe I never shall finish it. It was in vain that I took courage; it serves to little good in the execution of a thing almost impossible. I read a little of it with my master who tells me almost all the words, and, in fine, it makes me lose my time. I begin to have really great difficulty to write English; I wish I had some pretty letters to form my style. Pray tell me if it is certain that my sister comes in the month of July, because if it is, Madame De Taubenheim will keep a bed for her. My harpsichord is not come yet. Madame L'Abbesse is better, but she still keeps her bed. Madame De Taubenheim sends her compliments to you. Pray how does your arm go? I am very well now. Adieu, my dear papa; as I do not know any news, I must finish in assuring you of the sincerest affection of your loving child,

M. Jefferson.

My Dear Patsy   Nantes June 1. 1787.
Your letter of May 3. came to me at this place. Since this I
hear nothing from you; but I hope your health is reestab-
lished. I have received letters from America as late as March
assuring me that your sister shall be sent this summer. At
that time however they did not know certainly by what occasion she could come. There was a hope of getting her under
care of the French Consul and his lady, who thought of coming to France. The moment and place of her arrival therefore are still incertain. I forgot in my last letter to desire you
to learn all your old tunes over again perfectly, that I may
hear them on your harpsichord on it's arrival. I have no
news of it however since I left Paris, tho' presume it will arrive immediately as I had ordered. Learn some slow move-
ments of simple melody. . . . I am just setting out for Lori-
ent, and shall have the happiness of seeing you at Paris about
the 12th. or 15th. of this month, and of assuring you in person of the sincere love of your's affectionately,

                                        Th: Jefferson

In money matters Jefferson was always as generous to his
daughters as his means permitted. He sought to inculcate
in them the practice of thrift and of never buying anything unless they had the money in hand to pay for it.
He was apparently not too successful himself in following the principle he laid down for his daughters in this
next letter.

                                        Paris June 14. 1787.
I send you, my dear Patsy, the 15 livres you desired. you propose this to me as an anticipation of five weeks allowance.
but do you not see my dear how imprudent it is to lay out in
one moment what should accomodate you for five weeks?
That this is a departure from that rule which I wish to see

you governed by, thro' your whole life, of never buying any thing which you have not money in your pocket to pay for? be assured that it gives much more pain to the mind to be in debt, than to do without any article whatever which we may seem to want. the purchase you have made is one of those I am always ready to make for you, because it is my wish to see you dressed always cleanly & a little more than decently. but apply to me first for the money before you make a purchase, were it only to avoid breaking thro' your rule. learn yourself the habit of adhering vigorously to the rules you lay down for yourself. I will come for you about eleven o'clock on Saturday. hurry the making your gown, and also your reding-cote. You will go with me some day next week to dine at the Marquis Fayette's [Lafayette]. Adieu my dear daughter. Your's affectionately

Th: Jefferson

My Dear Patsy   Thursday June 28 [1787]
Madame de Traubenheim wrote me word yesterday that you were unwell. I shall come to Panthemont today to pay her a visit, and to bring you to dine, if well enough. Let me know by the bearer if you are well enough to come out. Make it a rule hereafter to come dressed otherwise than in your uniform. Our dear Polly was to sail certainly on the 1st. of May. She must therefore be arrived in England now. Adieu, my Dear, Yours affectionately,

Th: J.

Unknown to the worried father, Polly had already arrived in London, and Abigail Adams had two days before (June 26, 1787) written a letter to let Jefferson know of Polly's safe arrival. The longed-for reunion was now at hand. Petit was sent off to get Miss Polly; and within a

Paris June 14. 1787.

I send you, my dear Patsy, the 15 livres you desired. you propose this to me as an anticipation of five weeks allowance. but do you not see my dear how imprudent it is to lay out in one moment what should accomodate you for five weeks? that this is a departure from that rule which I wish to see you governed by, thro' your whole life, of never buying any thing which you have not money in your pocket to pay for? be assured that it gives much more pain to the mind to be in debt, than to do without any article whatever which we may seem to want. the purchase you have made is one of those I am always ready to make for you, because it is my wish to see you dressed always cleanly & a little more than decently. but apply to me first for the money before you make a purchase, were it only to avoid breaking thro' your rule. learn yourself the habit of adhering rigorously to the rules you lay down for yourself. I will come for you about eleven o'clock on Saturday. hurry the making your gown, and also your redingote. you will go with me some day next week to dine at the Marquis Fayette's. Adieu my dear daughter

yours affectionately

Th: Jefferson

Bitter financial problems were to cloud the last years of Jefferson's life. Yet he often urged prudent spending and thrift on his kinfolk, as he does here in this letter of June 14, 1787. (From Randall's Life of Jefferson, *1857.)*

month Polly was settled at the Panthemont school. Thus was the Jefferson family reunited.

Paris was then, and still is, a charming place for romance. In the summer of 1788, Martha's cousin Thomas Mann Randolph, Jr., came a-courting. He was a brilliant, versatile young man just graduated from the University of Edinburgh with honors. On his way home to Virginia he stopped off at Paris to call on the Jeffersons. No gallant whom Martha had met in Paris cut a finer dash than this tall, athletic, attentive young fellow. Perhaps it was the renewal of their childhood friendship, but most likely it was summertime in gay, flowery Paris. Randolph had not seen Martha since she was a gangling girl of ten; in Paris he found an elegant young lady of sixteen versed in all the graces. It was love at first sight, for apparently the two youthfuls plighted their troth under the spell of the enchanting city, though they kept it a secret until they met again in America.

Young Randolph was the oldest son of Thomas Mann Randolph, master of Tuckahoe on the James above Richmond. Randolph Senior and Jefferson were boyhood schoolmates when Peter Jefferson, Thomas' father, lived at Tuckahoe as guardian of the orphaned Randolphs. Martha's affianced was one of a promising group of American youths who, during Jefferson's stay in Paris, called often at the ministry for educational guidance.

In 1788, Jefferson had applied to the dying Confederation Congress for a six-month leave of absence, but nothing had come of it. His application had reached America at the height of the battles for ratification of the new Constitution, and nothing had come of it. After Washington's inauguration, Jefferson had renewed his plea. The first President complied promptly and in June, 1789, granted Jefferson's request. The news, however, did not reach Paris until August.

In late September, Jefferson said his last au revoir's to his many admiring friends, though events would prove

Martha, at sixteen, looked like the above when young Thomas Randolph fell in love with her that summer in Paris. In this miniature painted by Joseph Boze, Martha had reddish hair and blue eyes. (From the Wallace Collection, United States Embassy at Paris; courtesy of the U. S. Information Service.)

these should have been adieu's, and on October 8, the Jeffersons boarded a packet at Le Havre. With them went eighty-six huge packing cases stuffed with Jefferson's precious papers, architectural drawings, books, scores of odds and ends: plants, seeds, bits of sculpture, gold chairs, gold sofas, mirrors, paintings, and presents for the family back home. Not the least, but certainly the liveliest, item was a *"chienne bergère,* big with pup,'' whose progeny would gambol about Monticello to the end of Jefferson's days. At Cowes, Jefferson and his mountainous baggage were transferred to the *Clermont,* which on October 23 cleared for America. As Jefferson gazed back at the retreating shore he did not know he was having his last look at France, the "great and good country" he had learned to love.

He left behind him the opening fury of the French Revolution. In July, the grim old Bastille had fallen and the streets of Paris resounded with the cry *aux armes!* Fiery orators harangued the populace on every corner while gunfire crackled in the streets. Aristocrats fled the country in droves. From afar the guillotine was looming over King Louis XVI and Queen Marie Antoinette, the rulers who had guaranteed America's victory in *her* revolution by dispatching armies, munitions, and money to aid Washington's struggling Continentals.

A month's smooth sailing brought Jefferson to his native shore. Landing at Norfolk, he learned from a newspaper that President Washington had nominated him as the first Secretary of State of the United States. Traveling slowly, stopping often to visit old friends, the Jeffersons paused at Polly's beloved Eppington, where Aunt and Uncle Eppes and a bevy of young Eppeses rolled out a heart-warming welcome, including Maria's favorite cousin, Jack, for whom she had grieved when the big ship carried her off to France. Here an express rider overtook Jefferson with Washington's historic letter confirming his nomination to the high office.

But the voyage across the Atlantic, so peaceful and easy, had ended in near catastrophe. From Martha's pen we have a narrative of this exciting contretemps—the headwinds that almost overwhelmed their ship outside the Virginia capes and the fire that swept the vessel as it docked at Norfolk, threatening to consume their baggage with Jefferson's precious papers and the treasured accumulation of *objets d'art* of five years in France—and of the jubilation that greeted Jefferson and his two attractive daughters when on December 23 they stepped out of their carriage at Monticello—home at last.

The story goes that among those waiting to felicitate the wayfarers were two eager-eyed young gentlemen: Thomas Mann Randolph, Jr., who had hurried over from his father's upcountry estate, Edgehill, adjoining Monticello; and Jack Eppes, now a world-at-his-feet sixteen, and Maria's future husband, who handed the fairylike young lady out of the carriage with a flourish.

Jefferson hesitated before accepting the Chair of State at the cabinet table. France still called to his heart, and he received Washington's proffer with "real regret." After considerable soul-searching he replied in a masterly letter saying that although he preferred to return to the Paris station, he would, if Washington felt it best for the public welfare, accept the distinguished portfolio tendered him. He added, "It is not for an individual to choose his post," and thus he left to Washington the decision the nation wanted made.

"Cherish then for me, my dear child, the affection of your husband and continue to love me as you have done"

Hardly had Jefferson reached home in 1789 before Monticello began bustling with excitement over Martha's impending marriage to young Thomas Mann Randolph, Jr. The budding romance in Paris had come full bloom at Monticello. To Jefferson the match was most pleasing. With gusto he announced the engagement.

Few young men in Virginia held greater promise of future honors and accomplishments than Tom Randolph. Tall, graceful, intellectually gifted, he bore a distinguished name and had expectations of ample fortune. Martha herself possessed those qualities of head and heart that would endear her to all. Late in life her father spoke of her as "my dear and beloved daughter . . . the cherished companion of my early life and nurse of my age."

By mid-February the mansion was packed to the eaves with aunts, uncles, cousins, and in-laws, who came in droves for the wedding festivities. Yet, as was the custom of the day, before the happy couple took their vows the fathers had agreed on marriage settlements. Jefferson would endow Martha with one thousand acres of his Poplar Forest estate; Randolph Senior would deed to Tom his nine hundred-acre James River plantation, Varina. On February 23, 1790, Martha Jefferson, seventeen, was married to her second cousin, Tom Randolph, twenty, in the high entrance hall of Monticello. It was exactly two months to the day since the bride's homecoming after five years in France. The newlyweds dashed away for a short honeymoon and returned to Monticello, where they would stay until Jefferson arrived there from New York in the fall. Maria meantime would live at Eppington with the Eppeses and later rejoin her sister at Monticello.

With reluctance Jefferson had finally accepted the secretaryship in Washington's cabinet. He would later write a friend, "When I came into this office it was with the resolution to retire from it as soon as I could with decency." It meant separation from his children, with a tedious, bone-wearying ride intervening between the seat of government at New York and his beloved mountain home, which cried out for repairs after five years' neglect. While still in France, he had blueprinted improvements and innovations for Monticello, including a dome whose inspiration he drew from the dome of the Hotel de Salm in Paris though adapted along Palladian lines. He had looked forward joyfully to an architectural revelry remodeling his classic home.

On March 1, 1790, Jefferson grudgingly tore himself from family and home and headed for New York. After a harsh, wintry journey he arrived on March 21. Congress was in session and deeply embroiled over Alexander Hamilton's Assumption Bill, which Jefferson bitterly opposed but accepted in a log-rolling trade for the establishment of the nation's permanent capital on the banks of the Potomac.

Jefferson's letters to his daughters during his first years as Secretary of State reveal his fatherly concern for their welfare and an almost motherly love for them. Craving their constant affection, hungering for their companionship, he missed them poignantly during his long absences. Their letters seemed to sustain him. He once averred, "Public employment . . . is but honorable exile from one's family and affairs." Before embarking on his new post he had arranged a regular schedule for corresponding with his home folks. He would write every week. Martha was to answer one week; his son-in-law the next week; and Maria the week following. Martha and Tom followed this routine after a fashion, but Maria, unconsciously perhaps, bridled under it. She was always in his debt letterwise.

Jefferson thoughtfully addressed his first letter from New York to his son-in-law. He probably did this as a gesture of good will and in recognition of the young man as head of the family. Jefferson's first letter to Martha from his new post reflects a tinge of sadness. He seems a trifle fearful of being supplanted in her affections by his new son-in-law.

My Dear Daughter   New York April 4. 1790
I saw in Philadelphia your friends Mrs. Trist and Miss Rittenhouse. both complained of your not writing. in Baltimore
I enquired after mrs Buchanan and miss Holliday. the latter
is lately turned methodist, the former was married the evening I was there to a mr Turnbull of Petersburg in Virginia.
of course you will see her there. I find it difficult to procure
a tolerable house here. it seems it is a practice to let all the
houses the 1st. of February, & to enter into them the 1st of
May of course I was too late to engage one, at least in the
Broadway, where all my business lies. I have taken an indif-
ferent one nearly opposite mrs. Elsworth' which may give
me time to look about me & provide a better before the arrival of my furniture. I am anxious to hear from you, of your
health, your occupations, where you are &c. do not neglect
your music it will be a companion which will sweeten many
hours of life to you. I assure you mine here is triste enough.
having had yourself & dear Poll to live with me so long, to
exercise my affections and chear me in the intervals of business, I feel heavily the separation from you. it is a circumstance of consolation to know that you are happier; and to
see a prospect of it's continuance in the prudence and even
temper of both mr Randolph & yourself. your new condition
will call for abundance of little sacrifices. but they will be
greatly overpaid by the measure of affection they will secure
to you. the happiness of your life depends now on the continuing to please a single person. to this all other objects
must be secondary; even your love to me, were it possible
that that could ever be an obstacle. but this it can never be.
neither of you can ever have a more faithful friend than myself, nor one on whom you can count for more sacrifices. my
own is become a secondary object to the happiness of you
both. cherish then for me, my dear child, the affection of
your husband, and continue to love me as you have done,

and to render my life a blessing by the prospect it may hold up to me of seeing you happy. kiss Maria for me if she is with you, and present me cordially to mr Randolph: assuring yourself of the constant & unchangeable love of Your's affectionately,

Th. Jefferson

Martha's answer of April 25, 1790, was reassuring:

I assure you My Dear papa my happiness can never be compleat without your company Mr Randolph omits nothing that can in the least contribute to it. I have made it my study to please him in every *thing* and do consider all other objects as secondary to that *except* my love for you.

In the years ahead Martha would become a highly accomplished matron, and bear eleven grandchildren who would populate Monticello and Edgehill and bring untold happiness to their doting grandfather. Never beautiful like the exquisite Maria, she possessed rare traits of character. Poised, gifted in conversation and manners, she was her father's delight. It is not amiss to recall a distinguished occasion a few years later in Richmond, at which Martha Randolph's health was offered as the toasts went round. Among those present was eccentric John Randolph of Roanoke, now bitterly estranged from Jefferson. To the astonishment of all, Randolph suddenly rose, glass in hand, to utter in his shrill voice, "Yes, gentlemen, let us drink—to the noblest woman in Virginia."

Tom Randolph, however, did not quite live up to his youthful promise. Brilliant and talented though he was, Tom was improvident. His affairs, like those of his father-in-law, would in time become hopelessly involved. To add to his pecuniary misfortunes, he was not a man of easy temperament. Misfortune slowly drew off much of

Richmond April 25 1790

I received yours My Dearest Father with
more pleasure than is possible for me to express and am happy
to hear that you are at last settled at New Yorck as I am
in hopes we shall now hear from you often. we are just
returned from a visit up the country to aunt Carr and Mrs
Flemming's it has not been possible as yet to carry dear Pol
to Eppington for want of horses as Mr Randolph was
unwelling to borrow his father's for so long a time but I
expect certainly to be there in ten days, at latest. I
intend writing to Mrs Trist and Polly by the next
post and promiss you not to leave Richmond without
writing also to my friends in Europe. I hope you have
not given over comming to Virginia this fall as I
assure you My dear papa my happiness car never be
compleat without your company Mr Randolph omits
nothing that car in the least contribute to it I have
made it my study to please him in every thing and do

consider all other objects as secondary to that except my love for you—I do not know where we are to spend the summer Mr Randolph has some thoughts of settling at Varina for a little while till he can buy a part of Edgehill—I am much averse to it my self but shall certainly comply if he thinks it necessary My health is perfectly good as also dear Polly's. I have recieved a letter from Mrs Burson who informs me that the Duke of Dorset and Lady Caroline are both going to be married the former to a Miss Cope adieu My Dear Pappa I am with the tenderest affection yours

M. Randolph

Just eight weeks after her wedding, Martha wrote the above letter to her father. In it she warmly reassures "dear papa" that her "happiness can never be compleat" without his company. (Courtesy of the Massachusetts Historical Society.)

the warmer virtues of his younger days. Yet, in 1803, he was elected to the House of Representatives, in which he served two terms. In 1819 the people of Virginia elected him their governor. Time and time again, when cash was scarce at Edgehill, Jefferson came to the rescue of Martha Randolph's family. His account books attest his generosity to his beloved daughter. His own debts troubled him even more bitterly because they prevented his giving as much help to the Randolph family as he would have liked.

Martha's new state did not deter her loving father from continuing to write prescriptions for happiness and the good life. On April 26, 1790, he is writing:

Interesting occupations are essential to happiness: indeed the whole art of being happy consists in the art of finding emploiment. I know none so interesting, and which croud upon us so much, as those of a domestic nature. I look forward therefore to your commencing housekeepers on your own farm, with some anxiety. Till then you will not know how to fill up your time, and your weariness of the things around you will assume the form of a weariness of one another.

A few months later Martha found herself in the startling situation of having a new mother-in-law just her age— Randolph Senior, an elderly widower, had suddenly contracted a June-December wedding with a fair and fascinating young lady, Gabriella Harvie. Of course, Martha and Tom feared that the young bride might upset Tom's expectation of receiving Edgehill. On this domestic crisis, Jefferson wrote to Martha:

If the lady has anything difficult in her dispositions, avoid what is rough, and attach her good qualities to you. Consider what are otherwise as a bad stop in your harpsichord, and do not touch on it, but make yourself happy with the good ones. Every human being, my dear, must thus be viewed, according to what it is good for; for none of us, no not one, is perfect; and were we to love none who had imperfections, this world would be a desert for our love. All we can do is to make the best of our friends, love and cherish what is good in them, and keep out of the way of what is bad; but no more think of rejecting them for it, than of throwing away a piece of music for a flat passage or two. (July 17, 1790.)

> One could hardly blame Jefferson for pleading and scolding as he did in this self-explanatory letter. Bergere was a shepherd dog, the *"chienne bergère* big with pup," Jefferson brought overseas from France. Grizzle was her puppy. Bergere long held a place of affection at Monticello.

Philadelphia, Dec. 23d. 1790

My dear Daughter—This is a scolding letter for you all. I have not received a scrip of a pen from home since I left it. I think it so easy for you to write me one letter every week, which will be but once in the three weeks for each of you, when I write one every week, who have not one moment's repose from business, from the first to the last moment of the week.

Perhaps you think you have nothing to say to me. It is a great deal to say you are all well; or that one has a cold, another a fever, etc.; besides that, there is not a sprig of grass that shoots uninteresting to me; nor any thing that moves, from yourself down to Bergere or Grizzle. Write, then, dear daughter, punctually on your day, and Mr. Randolph and Polly on hers. I suspect you have news to tell me of yourself of the most tender interest to me. Why silent, then?

> Jefferson's surmise that something "of the most tender interest to me" was happening down at Monticello was

correct. Martha was nearing the day when she presented Jefferson with his first grandchild, a girl.

A baby girl named Anne Cary Randolph, born at Monticello in early 1791, ushered in a new and delightful era in Jefferson's life. When the joyful tidings from Monticello reached the new grandfather at Philadelphia, he sped off a letter of congratulations to the happy mother:

Your two last letters are those which have given me the greatest pleasure of any I ever received from you. The one announced that you were become a notable housewife; the other, a mother. This last is undoubtedly the keystone of the arch of matrimonial happiness, as the first is its daily aliment. (February 9, 1791.)

That May of 1791 Secretary of State Jefferson and Representative James Madison of Virginia jogged northward from Philadelphia to sample the beauties and fishing of lakes George and Champlain. They called this trip a "botanizing expedition." But the two statesmen had other fish to fry than those they hoped to catch in the lakes.

As they bumped along they hatched up plans for political war on Alexander Hamilton and his Federalists. At New York they paused to make a deal with a smart, handsome politician named Aaron Burr, Grand Sachem of the Sons of St. Tammany. In time these "sons" of the Indian patron saint would emerge politically as Tammany Hall.

From Lake Champlain Jefferson wrote glowing letters to his daughters. Engirdled with trees and set like a jewel in the mountains, Lake George, he said, surpassed any waters he had ever seen. But, he averred, the climate of New York State could not compare with that of Virginia whose climate was more delectable than anywhere else in the world.

Jefferson, always delighting in doing the out-of-the-ordinary, wrote these letters on sheets of birch bark. They are known as the "birch bark letters." Here is his letter to Martha.

Lake Champlain, May 31st, 1791.

My dear Martha—I wrote to Maria yesterday while sailing on Lake George, and the same kind of leisure is afforded me to-day to write to you. Lake George is, without comparison, the most beautiful water I ever saw; formed by a contour of mountains into a basin thirty-five miles long, and from two to four miles broad, finely interspersed with islands, its water limpid as crystal, and the mountain sides covered with rich groves of thuja, silver fir, white pine, aspen, and paper birch down to the water-edge; here and there precipices of rock to checker the scene and save it from monotony. An abundance of speckled trout, salmon trout, bass, and other fish, with which it is stored, have added, to our other amusements, the sport of taking them. Lake Champlain, though much larger, is a far less pleasant water. It is muddy, turbulent, and yields little game. After penetrating into it about twenty-five miles, we have been obliged, by a head wind and high sea, to return, having spent a day and a half in sailing on it. We shall take our route again through Lake George, pass through Vermont, down Connecticut River, and through Long Island to New York and Philadelphia. Our journey has hitherto been prosperous and pleasant, except as to the weather, which has been as sultry and hot through the whole as could be found in Carolina or Georgia. I suspect, indeed, that the heats of Northern climates may be more powerful than those of Southern ones in proportion as they are shorter. Perhaps vegetation requires this. There is as much fever and ague, too, and other bilious complaints on Lake Champlain as on the swamps of Carolina. Strawberries here are in the blossom, or just formed. With you, I sup-

pose, the season is over. On the whole, I find nothing anywhere else, in point of climate, which Virginia need envy
to any part of the world. Here they are locked up in ice and
snow for six months. Spring and autumn, which make a
paradise of our country, are rigorous winter with them; and
a tropical summer breaks on them all at once. When we consider how much climate contributes to the happiness of
our condition, by the fine sensations it excites, and the pro-
ductions it is the parent of, we have reason to value highly
the accident of birth in such a one as that of Virginia.

From this distance I can have little domestic to write to
you about. I must always repeat how much I love you. Kiss
the little Anne for me. I hope she grows lustily, enjoys good
health, and will make us all, and long, happy as the centre of
our common love. Adieu, my dear.

Yours affectionately,
Th. Jefferson.

Early in 1792 reflections of Jefferson's yearnings to retire from public life began to crop out in his letters home.
He had made up his mind to relinquish the cares of state
and return to Monticello. The only question was the tim-
ing. He was sick and tired, as he wrote James Madison,
"of giving up everything I love in exchange for everything I hate." No longer was he fascinated by the "hate-
ful occupation of politics" with its feuds, jealousies and
intrigues. But he was determined not to surrender his
high post under the fire of his political enemies.

His duel in the cabinet with Alexander Hamilton was
rising in intensity. Newspaper attacks on him were mounting. On top of it all he was eternally homesick. If he retired from office, he would do so decently, not under pressure. He decided to remain until the end of the year,
which, as he wrote Martha in one of his first letters home,
would be the "longest of my life," but he assured her
hopefully "the next we will sow our cabbages together."

My Dear Martha: Philadelphia, January 15th, 1792. Having no particular subject for a letter, I find none more soothing to my mind than to indulge itself in expressions of the love I bear you, and the delight with which I recall the various scenes through which we have passed together in our wanderings over the world. These reveries alleviate the toils and inquietudes of my present situation, and leave me always impressed with the desire of being at home once more, and of exchanging labor, envy and malice, for ease, domestic occupation and domestic love and society; where I may once more be happy with you, with Mr. Randolph and dear little Anne, with whom even Socrates might ride on a stick without being ridiculous. Indeed it is with difficulty that my resolution will bear me through what yet lies between the present day and that which, on mature consideration of all circumstances respecting myself and others, my mind has determined to be the proper one for relinquishing my office. Though not very distant, it is not near enough for my wishes. The ardor of these, however, would be abated, if I thought that on coming home I should be left alone. On the contrary, I hope that Mr. Randolph will find a convenience in making only leisurely preparations for a settlement, and that I shall be able to make you both happier than you have been at Monticello, and relieve you of *desagremens* to which I have been sensible you were exposed, without the power in myself to prevent it, but by my own presence. Remember me affectionately to Mr. Randolph, and be assured of the tender love of

Yours,
Th. Jefferson.

This summer of 1792, Jefferson and Maria reached Monticello in time for another blessed event, the arrival of a grandson, who was named for his loving grandfather, Thomas Jefferson Randolph. In time he would become all but a son to his grandsire. October saw Jefferson and Maria jogging north again to Philadelphia. By this time President Washington had consented to a second term. His earnest entreaties had likewise prevailed on Jefferson to reconsider and remain in the cabinet for a while at least.

Jefferson's memorable letter to Martha early in the New Year of 1793 reveals how reluctantly he postponed his retirement and at what sacrifice to his own interest and feelings. Yet he would wait until the last day of July before tendering his final resignation, which he couched in matchless rhetoric. He deferred his actual retirement until the last day of the year.

My Dear Martha: Philadelphia, January 26, 1793.
I received two days ago yours of the 16th. You were never more mistaken then in supposing you were too long on the prattle, etc., of little Anne. I read it with quite as much pleasure as you write it. I sincerely wish I could hear of her perfect reestablishment. I have for some time past been under an agitation of mind which I scarcely ever experienced before, produced by a check on my purpose of returning home at the close of this session of Congress. My operations at Monticello had been all made to bear upon that point of time; my mind was fixed on it with a fondness which was extreme, the purpose firmly declared to the President, when I became assailed from all quarters with a variety of objections. Among these it was urged that my retiring just when I had been attacked in the public papers, would injure me in the eyes of the public, who would suppose I either withdrew from investigation, or because I had not tone of mind sufficient to meet slander. The only reward I ever wished on my retirement was, to carry with me nothing like

a disapprobation of the public. These representations have for some weeks past shaken a determination which I have thought the whole world could not have shaken. I have not yet finally made up my mind on the subject, nor changed my declaration to the President. But having perfect reliance in the disinterested friendship of some of those who have counselled and urged it strongly; believing they can see and judge better a question between the public and myself than I can, I feel a possibility that I may be detained here into the summer. A few days will decide. . . .

In December, 1793, Jefferson made the move that he had been yearning to make for two long years—he retired from Washington's cabinet and, he hoped, from the political arena. Pressures too powerful to be withstood had prevailed on him to defer carrying out his decision. But by December 22, 1793, he is writing to Martha firmly, "The President made yesterday, what I hope will be the last set at me to continue; but in this I am now immovable by any considerations whatever."

Jefferson fondly imagined he had come home to stay, aloof from a busy world. Now he could devote his time to architecture and farming and the family he loved so dearly. He had seemingly reached his paradise.

For three short years he was allowed to live his days as he yearned to. He busied himself with his crops, alterations to Monticello, and Martha's growing brood of small ones. Another young Randolph, Ellen Wayles, arrived in those years. Tom and Martha were now living at nearby Edgehill, with occasional visits to Varina, their plantation on the James below Richmond, and Polly spent much of her time at Monticello.

But Jefferson's dream of retiring from the political maelstrom to the "enjoyment of my farm, my family & my books" was rudely shattered in November, 1796, by his election to the vice-presidency. In late February, 1797, he journeyed north to Philadelphia to plunge again into the world of politics. But his heart stayed at Monticello with the family he loved.

Early in his second year as Vice President, he writes wearily, in a letter to Martha:

I ought oftener, my dear Martha, to receive your letters, for the very great pleasure they give me, and especially when they express your affections for me; for, though I can not doubt them, yet they are among those truths which, though not doubted, we love to hear repeated. Here, too, they serve, like gleams of light, to cheer a dreary scene; where envy, hatred, malice, revenge, and all the worst passions of men, are marshalled to make one another as miserable as possible. I turn from this with pleasure, to contrast it with your fireside, where the single evening I passed at it was worth more than ages here. Indeed, I find myself detaching very fast, perhaps too fast, from every thing but yourself, your sister, and those who are identified with you. These form the last hold the world will have on me, the cords which will be cut only when I am loosened from this state of being. (February 8, 1798.)

Even the coming of spring made him no more fond of the political life. To Martha, he writes:

For you to feel all the happiness of your quiet situation, you should know the rancorous passions which tear every breast here, even of the sex which should be a stranger to them. Politics and party hatreds destroy the happiness of every being here. They seem, like salamanders, to consider fire as their element. (May 17, 1798.)

The end of his term as Vice President brought no surcease to Jefferson. At the will of the Democratic-Republican party he had fathered, Jefferson ran against his old friend and Federalist, John Adams, for the presidency in the election of 1800, which produced the first tie for the presidency in American history. Jefferson and his running mate, Aaron Burr, each garnered seventy-three electoral votes, thus throwing the issue into the House of Representatives. In late January, 1801, barely a fortnight before the House was to meet to break the tie, Jefferson wrote Martha an unusual letter. Ruminating on his chances of becoming President, he seemed to attach as much importance to the fact that Washington, the nation's new capital, was "but three easy days' journey" from Monticello and his family as to his hope of winning the presidency.

But he added a significant postscript: Alexander Hamilton, his political enemy, was using his "uttermost influence" to elect him over Burr.

Washington, January 26, 1801.

My Dear Martha,— . . . I long to be in the midst of the children, and have more pleasure in their little follies than in the wisdom of the wise. Here, too, there is such a mixture of the bad passions of the heart, that one feels themselves in an enemy's country. It is an unpleasant circumstance, if I am destined to stay here, that the great proportion of those of the place who figure are Federalists, and most of them of the violent kind. Some have been so personally bitter that they can never forgive me, though I do them with sincerity. Perhaps in time they will get tamed. Our prospect as to the election has been alarming; as a strong disposition exists to prevent an election, and that case not being provided for by the Constitution, a dissolution of the government seemed possible. At present there is a prospect that some, though Federalists, will prefer yielding to the wishes of the people rather than have no government. If I am fixed here, it will be but three easy days' journey from you, so that I should hope you and the family could pay an annual visit here at least; which with mine to Monticello of the spring and fall, might enable us to be together four or five months of the year. On this subject, however, we may hearafter converse, lest we should be counting chickens before they are hatched. I inclose for Anne a story, too long to be got by heart but worth reading. Kiss them all for me, and keep them in mind of me. Tell Ellen I am afraid she has forgotten me. I shall probably be with you the first week in April, as I shall endeavor to be at our court for that month. Continue to love me, my dear Martha, and be assured of my unalterable and tenderest love to you. Adieu.

[Thomas Jefferson]

P.S. Hamilton is using his uttermost influence to procure my election rather than Colonel Burr's.

Seven years later he wrote wearily to Martha:

But I am tired of a life of contention and of being the personal object for the hatred of every man who hates the present state of things. I long to be among you, where I know nothing but love and delight, and where instead of being chained to a writing table I could be indulged as others are with the blessings of domestic society and pursuits of my own choice. (November 23, 1807.)

On March 4, 1809 the longed-for reprieve came. Having held the highest offices his country could offer him, having devoted almost four decades to the building of a new nation and in the service of his country, the sixty-six-year-old Jefferson returned to the life of a Virginia farmer. Almost two decades in the heart of the family he loved lay ahead of the "Sage of Monticello." He believed he "could be indulged as others are with the blessings of domestic society and pursuits of my own choice." In this he was to be disappointed.

I I

Mary Jefferson

1 7 7 8 - 1 8 0 4

*"You shall have as many dolls and play-
things as you want"*

My dear Papa: I want to know what day you are going to
come and see me, and if you will bring sister Patsy and my
baby [doll] with you. I was glad of my sashes and gave cousin Bolling one. I can almost read.

Your affectionate daughter,
Polly Jefferson

Such was the brief missive (by Aunt Eppes' hand) Polly
Jefferson wrote early in 1784 to her father, then in Annapolis at the Confederation Congress. Her spirited in-
quiry when she might expect a visit from him must have
amused her adoring parent considerably.

Eppington was bright with spring flowers when the post brought Jefferson's reply. It was addressed to Mrs. Elizabeth Eppes, but contained many messages for Polly: he and Martha were taking a "big boat" for France. She must be a good girl, mind her Aunt Eppes, be good to her little sister, Lucy, and love everybody at Eppington including her five little cousins. And very necessary, she must write to him regularly. This last injunction was imperative. All her too-brief life Polly was a reluctant letter-writer. She certainly did not inherit her father's fluent pen. In later years he would often implore her to write him, if only a few lines to let him know she was well and happy. Dutifully Polly would sharpen her quill, open her inkpot and sandbox, but words just refused to take shape. She really never learned to write letters, yet her beauty was to make amends for her shortcomings in literary achievement.

It is doubtful if Polly realized what a distinguished man her father was, and her notions of Paris were probably equally hazy.

Hardly was Martha settled at the Panthemont school in Paris when Jefferson received a letter from Elizabeth Eppes that wrung his heart. Little Lucy, just two, was gone. With her went the Eppes' own little Lucy. With tender sensibility Mrs. Eppes broke the sad news.

To Jefferson, the old griefs came surging back. For days he was reduced almost to melancholia. Of his six children only two daughters survived, and fears for Polly now assailed him. "My dear little Polly hangs on my thoughts night and day," he wrote to Mrs. Eppes. He determined that Polly must join him and Martha in Paris, though his heart trembled at the idea of committing her to the whims and perils of an ocean voyage. So he wrote, "I drop my pen at the thought, but she must come." He did not want Polly to grow up a stranger to her father and sister. Happy as she was at Eppington, beloved by her Aunt and

Uncle Eppes and her cousins, particularly Jacky, he feared her affections would unconsciously be weaned away from him. "It is of importance to the future happiness of the child that she should neither forget nor be forgotten by her sister and myself."

Late in the summer of 1785 he wrote Francis Eppes minute instructions for Polly's journey to Paris. She must sail between the months of April and July, thus avoiding the equinoctial storms; the vessel that bore her must be less than five years old and have made at least one crossing; a trustworthy Negro woman must accompany her. He would expect her next summer. "My anxieties on this subject could induce me to endless detail, but your discretion and that of Mrs. Eppes saves me the necessity. . . . I would rather live a year longer without her than have her trusted to any but a good ship and a summer passage."

It was quite disturbing to the Eppeses who now loved Polly as one of their own. Polly herself stamped her little heel and simply refused to go. Even at seven she knew her own mind. Jefferson followed up his instructions with a letter to Polly herself, coaxing her to join him.

Paris, Sept. 20th, 1785.

My dear Polly—I have not received a letter from you since I came to France. If you knew how much I love you and what pleasure the receipt of your letters gave me at Philadelphia, you would have written to me, or at least have told your aunt what to write, and her goodness would have induced her to take the trouble of writing it. I wish so much to see you, that I have desired your uncle and aunt to send you to me. I know, my dear Polly, how sorry you will be, and ought to be, to leave them and your cousins; but your sister and myself can not live without you, and after a while we will carry you back again to see your friends in Virginia. In

the mean time you shall be taught here to play on the harpsichord, to draw, to dance, to read and talk French, and
such other things as will make you more worthy of the love
of your friends; but above all things, by our care and love of
you, we will teach you to love us more than you will do if you
stay so far from us. I have had no opportunity since Colonel
Le Maire went, to send you anything; but when you come
here you shall have as many dolls and playthings as you want
for yourself, or to send to your cousins whenever you shall
have opportunities. I hope you are a very good girl, that you
love your uncle and aunt very much, and are very thankful
to them for all their goodness to you; that you never suffer
yourself to be angry with any body, that you give your playthings to those who want them, that you do whatever any
body desires of you that is right, that you never tell stories,
never beg for any thing, mind your books and your work
when your aunt tells you, never play but when she permits
you, nor go where she forbids you; remember, too, as a constant charge, not to go out without your bonnet, because it
will make you very ugly, and then we shall not love you so
much. If you always practice these lessons we shall continue
to love you as we do now, and it is impossible to love you
more. We shall hope to have you with us next summer, to
find you a very good girl, and to assure you of the truth of
our affection for you. Adieu, my dear child! Your's affectionately,

Th. Jefferson

But Polly was unmoved. She replied with a brief note
that added up to a positive, No! She longed to see him
but she did not want to go to France. Her warm clinging
nature rebelled at the very idea of leaving Aunt Eppes.
All his life, Jefferson cherished this little keepsake and
two others written in Polly's childish scrawl.

Eppington on the James 1785
Dear Papa—I long to see you, and hope that you and sister
Patsy are well; give my love to her and tell her that I long
to see her, and hope that you and she will come very soon to
see us. I hope that you will send me a doll. I am very sorry
that you have sent for me. I don't want to go to France, I had
rather stay with Aunt Eppes. Aunt Carr, Aunt Nancy and
Cousin Polly Carr are here. Your most happy and dutiful
daughter,

Polly Jefferson

Dear Papa—I should be very happy to see you, but I can not
go to France, and hope that you and sister Patsy are well.
Your affectionate daughter. Adieu.

Mary Jefferson

Dear Papa—I want to see you and sister Patsy, but you must
come to Uncle Eppes's house.

Polly Jefferson

The summer of 1786 came and went but Polly did not
embark for France. Uncle Eppes failed to find a suitable
ship; most likely he didn't want to. Elizabeth Eppes
frankly wrote Jefferson she was hoping each day would
bring a letter countermanding his orders to send Polly to
Paris. They had used every "stratagem" to prevail on
Polly to consent to the journey, but to no avail. Her own
children, she wrote, would gladly take her place "for the
number of things she is promised."

In May, 1787, Uncle Eppes quietly engaged passage for
Polly and her teen-age Negro maid, Sally Hemings, on a
good, stout ship, mastered by Captain Ramsey, a hardy
veteran of the sea, who was quite taken with the idea of
fetching Thomas Jefferson's daughter across the Atlantic.

But the pretty little passenger-to-be refused to go willingly; and the Eppeses reluctantly resorted to a ruse.

Captain Ramsey sailed his ship up the James River and moored it at Osborne's plantation, not far from Eppington. So excited were the young folk that Aunt Eppes took them over to see the big ship, frolic about the deck, and meet brave Captain Ramsey. Polly's trunks and bags were meanwhile smuggled aboard, and the children, after romping and racing about the ship, were all scurried off to a cabin to take a nap. As soon as Polly was fast asleep the Eppes youngsters were quietly whisked ashore, Captain Ramsey cast off, and when Polly opened her eyes she was on her way to Paris.

On June 26, 1787, after a fast, stormless passage, Captain Ramsey appeared at the American ministry in London holding the hand of an adorable little girl who was all smiles and whom he delivered to Abigail Adams, wife of John Adams, American minister plenipotentiary to the Court of St. James's. That same day Mrs. Adams hurried off an express letter to Jefferson announcing Polly's arrival.

My Dear Sir   London june 26 1787
I have to congratulate you upon the safe arrival of your Little Daughter, whom I have only a few moments ago received. She is in fine Health and a Lovely little Girl I am sure from her countanance, but at present every thing is strange to her, and she was very loth to try New Friends for old. She was so much attachd to the Captain and he to her, that it was with no small regret that I seperated her from him, but I dare say I shall reconcile her in a day or two. I tell her that I did not see her sister cry once. She replies that her sister was older and ought to do better, besides she had pappa with her. I shew her your picture. She says she cannot know it, how,

should she when she should not know you. A few hours acquaintance and we shall be quite Friends I dare say. I have so strong an inducement to tempt you. If you could bring Miss Jefferson with you, it would reconcile her little Sister to the thoughts of taking a journey. It would be proper that some person should be accustomed to her. The old Nurse whom you expected to have attended her, was sick and unable to come. She has a Girl about 15 or 16 with her, the Sister of the Servant you have with you. As I presume you have but just returnd from your late excursion, you will not put yourself to any inconvenience or Hurry in comeing or sending for her. You may rely upon every attention towards her and every care in my power. I have just endeavourd to amuse her by telling her that I would carry her to Sadlers Wells. After describing the amusement to her with an honest simplicity, I had rather says she see captain Ramsey one moment, than all the fun in the World.

I have only time before the post goes, to present my compliments to Mr. Short. Mr. Adams and Mrs. Smith desire to be rememberd to you. Captain Ramsey has brought a Number of Letters. As they may be of importance to you to receive them we have forwarded them by the post. Miss Polly sends her duty to you and Love to her Sister and says she will try to be good and not cry. So she has wiped her eyes and layd down to sleep.

Believe me dear Sir affectionately yours &c &c,

A Adams

Dear Sir   London june 27 1787
I had the Honour of addressing you yesterday and informing you of the safe arrival of your daughter. She was but just come when I sent of my letter by the post, and the poor little Girl was very unhappy being wholy left to strangers. This however lasted only a few Hours, and Miss is as contented to

day as she was misirable yesterday. She is indeed a fine child. I have taken her out to day and purchased her a few articles which she could not well do without and I hope they will meet your approbation. The Girl who is with her is quite a child, and Captain Ramsey is of opinion will be of so little Service that he had better carry her back with him. But of this you will be a judge. She seems fond of the child and appears good naturd. . . .

A. Adams

Jefferson hastened to write to Abigail.

Paris July 1. 1787.

A thousand thanks to you, my dear Madam, for your kind attention to my little daughter. Her distresses I am sure must have been troublesome to you: but I know your goodness will forgive her, and forgive me too for having brought them on you. Petit [Jefferson's steward] now comes for her. By this time she will have learned again to love the hand that feeds and comforts her, and have formed an attachment to you. She will think I am made only to tear her from all her affections. I wish I could have come myself. The pleasure of a visit to yourself and Mr. Adams would have been a great additional inducement. But, just returned from my journey, I have the arrearages of 3. or 4. months all crouded on me at once. I do not presume to write you news from America, because you have it so much fresher and frequenter than I have. . . .

Jefferson promptly dispatched his trusty steward Adrien Petit to London to escort Polly to Paris. By the time Petit arrived Mrs. Adams' little guest had become so attached to that estimable lady that another tearful good-by scene ensued. Again Polly had to be decoyed into leaving.

Jefferson's next letter crossed the following from Abigail Adams, both written the same day.

Dear Sir   London july 10th. 1787
When I wrote you last I did not know that petit had taken
places in the Stage and paid for them. This being the case I
have represented it to your little daughter and endeavourd
to prevail with her to consent to going at the time appointed.
She says if I must go I will, but I cannot help crying so pray
dont ask me to. I should have taken great pleasure in presenting her to you here, as you would then have seen her
with her most engageing countanance. Several lines of an old
song frequently occur to me as different objects affect her.

> What she thinks in her Heart
> You may read in her Eyes
> For knowing no art
> She needs no disguise.

I never saw so intelligent a countanance in a child before,
and the pleasure she has given me is an ample compensation
for any little services I have been able to render her. I can
easily conceive the earnest desire you must have to embrace
so lovely a child after so long a separation from her. That
motive, and my own intention of setting out next week upon
a journey into the County of Devonshire, has prevaild with
me to consent to parting with her so soon, but most reluctantly I assure you. Her temper, her disposition, her sensibility are all formed to delight. Yet perhaps at your first in-
terview you may find a little roughness but it all subsides in
a very little time, and she is soon attached by kindness. I inclose a memorandum of the articles purchased . . . that you
might know how I [spent] the money. . . . You will be so
good as to let me hear from my dear little Girl by the first

71

post after her arrival. My Love to her sister whom I congratulate upon such an acquisition. . . .

A Adams

Three days before her ninth birthday Polly reached Paris to meet two people—her father and sister Martha—whom she hardly recognized. Nor would they have known her perhaps, but for Captain Ramsey's assurance, via Mrs. Adams, that this was the young girl Mrs. Eppes had entrusted to his safekeeping. Polly was soon established at the Panthemont school with her sister. She quickly became a favorite with her French companions who first called her *Mademoiselle Polie,* only later to gallicize her given name Mary into Marie, which clung to her until she returned to America where it was remodeled into Maria, the name she bore to the close of her life.

"Be good, my dear . . . and all the world
will love you, and I more than all
the world"

The new Secretary of State waited until April 11, 1790, before writing his first letter from New York to pretty little Miss Maria. Jefferson was obviously disturbed not hearing from her though he tried often to view it in a humorous light. Her long silences sometimes reduced him to despair. His anxiety was increased by knowing how frail she was.

Now nearing thirteen, Maria was already a fresh young beauty. No likeness of her has ever come to light, but her resemblance to her delicate mother is supposed to have induced Jefferson's special tenderness toward her. He perhaps feared he would lose her as he had lost her mother, her three sisters, and a brother.

Three more weeks went by with no word from Maria, so Jefferson wrote again complaining that Maria owed him two letters, but, even so, she must make him a pudding when he came home on his vacation late in September. He used various devices to lure letters from her, often plying her with questions about the gardens, crops and birds around Monticello. What about the swallows and whippoorwills and chickens? And the peas and strawberries? How was the weather on his little mountain? But Maria failed to share her father's enthusiasm for meteorological subjects, such as comparing the climates of New York and Monticello. He even proposed making her his "botanical and zoological correspondent," but that worked out none too well. Maria was seldom in the mood for botany or zoology or writing letters. During Maria's stay at Eppington this summer of 1790, Jefferson even threatened to write her Aunt Eppes to make her go without her dinner until she answered his letters.

New York Apr. 11. 1790

Where are you, my dear Maria? How do you do? How are you occupied? Write me a letter by the first post and answer me all these questions. Tell me whether you see the sun rise every day? How many pages a-day you read in Don Quixot? How far you are advanced in him? Whether you repeat a Grammar lesson every day? What else you read? How many hours a day you sew? Whether you have an opportunity of continuing your music? Whether you know how to make a pudding yet, to cut out a beef stake, to sow spinach? Or to set a hen? Be good, my dear, as I have always found you, never be angry with any body, nor speak harm of them, try to let every body's faults be forgotten, as you would wish yours to be; take more pleasure in giving what is best to another than in having it yourself, and then all the world will love you, and I more than all the world. If your sister is with you kiss her and tell her how much I love her also, and present my affections to Mr. Randolph. Love your Aunt and Uncle, and be dutiful and obliging to them for all their kindness to you. What would you do without them, and with such a vagrant for a father? Say to both of them a thousand affectionate things for me: and Adieu my dear Maria,

Th: Jefferson

My Dear Papa   Richmond, April 25th, 1790
I am afraid you will be displeased in knowing where I am, but I hope you will not, as Mr. Randolph certainly had some good reason, though I do not know it. I have not been able to read in don quixote every day, as I have been travelling ever since I saw you last, and the dictionary is too large to go in the pocket of the chariot, nor have I yet had an opportunity of continuing my music. I am now reading robertson's america. I thank you for the advice you were so good as to give me, and will try to follow it. Adieu, my dear papa. I am your affectionate daughter,

Maria Jefferson

Maria's letter had not yet reached him so he wrote again.

My Dear Maria   New York May 2. 1790
I wrote to you three weeks ago, and have not yet received an answer. I hope however that one is on the way and that I shall receive it by the first post. I think it very long to have been absent from Virginia two months and not to have received a line either from yourself, your sister or Mr. Randolph, and I am very uneasy at it. As I write once a week to one or the other of you in turn, if you would answer my letter the day or day after you receive it, it would always come to my hands before I write the next to you.—We had two days of snow about the beginning of last week. Let me know

if it snowed where you are. I send you some prints of a new kind for your amusement. I send several to enable you to be generous to your friends. I want much to hear how you employ yourself. Present my best affections to your uncle, aunt and cousins, if you are with them, or to Mr. Randolph and your sister if with them: be assured of my tender love to you, and continue yours to your affectionate,

Th: Jefferson

Dear Papa   Eppington May 23 [1790]
I received your affectionate letter when I was at presqu'isle but was not able to answer it before I came here as the next day we went to uncle Bolings and then came here I thank you for the pictures you was so kind as to send me and will try that your advise shall not be thrown away. I read in don quixote every day to my aunt and say my grammer in spanish and english and write and read in robertson's america after I am done that I work till dinner and a little more after It did not snow at all last month my cousin Boling and myself made a pudding the other day my aunt has given us a hen and chickens adieu my Dear papa. Believe me to be your ever dutiful and affetionate daughter,

Maria Jefferson

My Dear Maria   New York May 23. 1790
I was glad to receive your letter of April 25. because I had been near two months without hearing from any of you. I hope you will now always write immediately on receiving a letter from me. Your last told me what you were not doing: that you were not reading Don Quixote, not applying to your music. I hope your next will tell me what you are doing. Tell your Uncle that the President after having been so ill as at one time to be thought dying, is now quite recovered.

I have been these three weeks confined by a periodical headach. It has been the most moderate I ever had: but it has not yet left me. Present my best affections to your Uncle and aunt. Tell the latter I shall never have thanks enough for her kindness to you, and that you will repay her in love and duty. Adieu my dear Maria.
Your's affectionately,

Th: Jefferson

My Dear Maria   New York June 13. 1790
I have recieved your letter of May 23. which was in answer to mine of May 2. but I wrote you also on the 23d. of May, so that you still owe me an answer to that, which I hope is now on the road. In matters of correspondence as well as of money you must never be in debt. I am much pleased with the account you give me of your occupations, and the making the pudding is as good an article of them as any. When I come to Virginia I shall insist on eating a pudding of your own making, as well as on trying other specimens of your skill. You must make the most of your time while you are with so good an aunt who can learn you every thing. We had not peas nor strawberries here till the 8th. day of this month. On the same day I heard the first whip-poor-will whistle. Swallows and martins appeared here on the 21st. of April. When did they appear with you? And when had you peas, strawberries, and whip-poor-wills in Virginia? Take notice hereafter whether the whip-poor-wills always come with the strawberries and peas. Send me a copy of the maxims I gave you, also a list of the books I promised you. I have had a long touch of my periodical headache, but a very moderate one. It has not quite left me yet. Adieu, my dear, love your uncle, aunt and cousins, and me more than all. Your's affectionately,

Th: Jefferson

New York July 4. 1790

I have written you, my dear Maria, four letters since I have been here, and I have received from you only two. You owe me two then, and the present will make three. This is a kind of debt I will not give up. You may ask how I will help myself? By petitioning your aunt, as soon as you receive a letter to make you go without your dinner till you have answered it. How goes on the Spanish? How many chickens have you raised this summer? Send me a list of the books I have promised you at different times, tell me what sort of weather you have had, what sort of crops are likely to be made, how your uncle and aunt, and the family do, and how you do yourself. I shall see you in September for a short time. Adieu, my dear Poll. Yours affectionately,

Th: Jefferson

Eppington, July 20th, 1790

Dear Papa—I hope you will excuse my not writing to you before, though I have none for myself. I am very sorry to hear that you have been sick, but flatter myself that it is over. My aunt Skipwith has been very sick, but she is better now; we have been to see her two or three times. You tell me in your last letter that you will see me in September, but I have received a letter from my brother [in-law] that says you will not be here before February; as his is later than yours, I am afraid you have changed your mind. The books that you have promised me are Anacharsis and Gibbon's Roman Empire. If you are coming in September, I hope you will not forget your promise of buying new jacks for the piano-forte that is at Monticello. Adieu, my dear papa.

I am your affectionate daughter,

Mary Jefferson

Dear Papa   Eppington may 23

I received your affectionate
letter when I was at prequ'ile but
was not able to answer it before I came
here as the next day we went to uncle
Bolings and then came here I thank
you for the pictures you was so kind
as to send me and will try that your
advise shall not be thrown away I
read in don quixote every day to my
aunt and say a my gramer in spanish
and english and write and read in
robertson's america after I am done that
I work till dinner and a little more

Jefferson Maria
rec'd June 5. 1790

after it did not snow atall last month
my cousin Boling and myself made a
pudding the otherday my aunt has given
us a hen and chickens adieu my
Dear papa believe me to be your ever
dutiful and affetionate daughter
Maria Jefferson

Here Maria, twelve, writes of her intention to heed her father's advice—to study hard and excel in the fine arts. Jefferson made it a habit—as he did in this letter of May 23, 1790—to add the date of arrival to all the correspondence he received (see upper right). (Courtesy of Dr. Robert H. Kean, Charlottesville, Virginia.)

Dear Papa   [Received Aug. 28, 1790]
I have just received your last favour july 23 and am determined to write to you every day till I have discharged my
debt when we were in Cumberland we went to Church and
heard some singing Masters that sung very well they are to
come here to learn my cousins to sing and as I know you
have no objections to my learning any thing I am to be a
scholar and hope to give you the pleasure of hearing an an-
them we had pease the 14 of may and strawberries the 17 of
the same month tho not in that abundance we are accustomed to in consequence of a frost this spring as for the martins swallows and whippoorwills I was so taken up with my
chickens that I never attended to them and therefore cannot
tell you when they came tho I was so unfortunate as to lose
half of them for my cousin Bolling and myself have raised
but 13 between us adieu my Dear Papa
                          believe me to be your affectionate daughter
                                                        Mary Jefferson

Jefferson arrived at Monticello in late September, but December found him back at his cabinet post in Philadelphia (the new temporary capital) and still endeavoring to
persuade Maria to adopt some sort of regular timetable
for writing to him.

My Dear Poll: Philadelphia, Dec. 7, 1790.
This week I write to you, and if you answer my letter as soon
as you receive it, and send it to Colonel Bell at Charlottesville, I shall receive it the day before I write to you again
—that will be three weeks hence; and this I shall expect you
to do always, so that by the correspondence of Mr. Randolph,
your sister, and yourself, I may hear from home once a week.
Mr. Randolph's letter from Richmond came to me about five
days ago. How do you all do? Tell me that in your letter, also

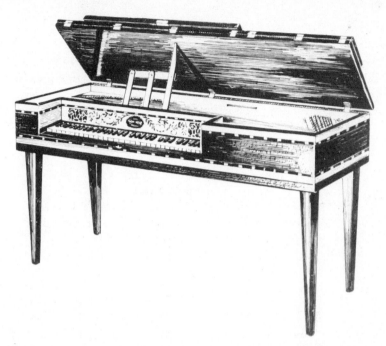

"Inform me what books you read, what tunes you learn," wrote Jeffer-son to eleven-year-old Patsy on November 28, 1783. Even at an early age, Jefferson tried to instill a love of the arts in his children and grandchil-dren. This is Jefferson's pianoforte at Monticello.

what is going forward with you, how you employ yourself, what weather you have had. We have already had two or three snows here. The workmen are so slow in finishing the house I have rented here, that I know not when I shall have it ready, except one room which they promise me this week, and which will be my bedroom, study, dining-room, and parlor. I am not able to give any later news about peace or war than of October 16th, which I mentioned in my last to your sister. Wheat has fallen a few pence, and will, I think, continue to fall, slowly at first and rapidly after a while. Adieu, my dear Maria; kiss your sister for me, and assure

Mr. Randolph of my affection. I will not tell you how much I love you, lest by rendering you vain, it might render you less worthy of my love.

Encore adieu,
Th. J

> The big event of 1791 in Jefferson's circle was, of course, the arrival of his first grandchild, Anne Cary Randolph. Jefferson's correspondence with Maria after the event opened with a scolding, but his jovial mood came bubbling out in a later letter he wrote to "Aunt Maria," as he dubbed her after little Anne came on the scene.

Philadelphia, Jan. 5th, 1791.

I did not write to you, my dear Poll, the last week, because I was really angry at receiving no letter. I have now been near nine weeks from home, and have never had a scrip of a pen, when by the regularity of the post I might receive your letters as frequently and as exactly as if I were at Charlottesville. I ascribed it at first to indolence, but the affection must be weak which is so long overruled by that. Adieu.

Th. J.

Monticello, January 22d, 1791.

Dear Papa—I received your letter of December the 7th about a fortnight ago, and would have answered it directly, but my sister had to answer hers last week and I this. We are all well at present. Jenny Randolph and myself keep house—she one week, and I the other. I owe sister thirty-five pages in Don Quixote, and am now paying them as fast as I can. Last Christmas I gave sister the "Tales of the Castle," and she made me a present of the "Observer," a little ivory box, and one of her drawings; and to Jenny she gave "Paradise Lost," and some other things. Adieu, dear Papa. I am your affectionate daughter,

Maria Jefferson.

Dear Papa   February 13 [1791]
I am very sorry that my not having wrote to you before made you doubt of my affection towards you and hope that after having read my last letter you were not so displeased as at first. in my last I said that my sister was very well but she was not she had been very sick all day without my knowing any thing of it as I stayed upstairs the whole day however she is very well now and the little one also she is very pretty has beautiful deep blue eyes and is a very fine child Adieu my Dear Papa beleive me to be your affectionate daughter

Mary Jefferson

Philadelphia, February 16th, 1791.
My dear Poll—At length I have recieved a letter from you. as the spell is now broke, I hope you will continue to write every three weeks. observe I do not admit the excuse you make of not writing because your sister had not written the week before; let each write their own week without regard to what others do, or do not do. I congratulate you my dear aunt on your new title. I hope you pay a great deal of attention to your niece, and that you have begun to give her lessons on the Harpsichord, in Spanish etc. tell your sister I make her a present of Gregory's Comparative View, inclosed herewith, and that she will find in it a great deal of useful advice for a young mother. I hope herself & the child are well. Kiss them both for me. Present me affectionately to mr. Randolph & miss Jenny. mind your Spanish & your Harpsichord well, and think often & always of,

yours affectionately
Th: Jefferson.
P.S.—Letter inclosed, with the book for your sister.

Philadelphia, March 9th, 1791.

My dear Maria—I am happy at length to have a letter of yours to answer, for that which you wrote to me February 13th came to hand February 28th. I hope our correspondence will now be more regular, that you will be no more lazy, and I no more in the pouts on that account. On the 27th of February I saw blackbirds and robin-redbreasts, and on the 7th of this month I heard frogs for the first time this year. Have you noted the first appearance of these things at Monticello? I hope you have, and will continue to note every appearance, animal and vegetable, which indicates the approach of spring, and will communicate them to me. By these means we shall be able to compare the climates of Philadelphia and Monticello. Tell me when you shall have peas, etc., up; when every thing comes to table; when you shall have the first chickens hatched; when every kind of tree blossoms, or puts forth leaves; when each kind of flower blooms. Kiss your sister and niece for me, and present me affectionately to Mr. Randolph and Miss Jenny.

Yours tenderly, my dear Maria,
Th. J.

Philadelphia, March 31st, 1791.

My dear Maria—I am happy to have a letter of yours to an-swer. That of March 6th came to my hands on the 24th. By-the-by, you never acknowledged the receipt of my letters, nor tell me on what day they came to hand. I presume that by this time you have received the two dressing-tables with marble tops. I give one of them to your sister, and the other to you: mine is here with the top broken in two. Mr. Ran-dolph's letter, referring to me the name of your niece, was very long on the road. I answered it as soon as I received it, and hope the answer got duly to hand. Lest it should have been delayed, I repeated last week to your sister the name of

My dear Poll   Philadelphia Feb. 16. 1791.   8

At length I have recieved a letter from you. as the
spell is now broke, I hope you will continue to write every three
weeks. observe I do not admit the excuse you make of not
writing because your sister had not written the week before:
let each write their own week without regard to what others.
do, or do not do.   I congratulate you my dear aunt on
your new title.   I hope you pay a great deal of attention
to your niece, and that you have begun to give her lessons
on the Harpsichord, in Spanish &c.   tell your sister I
make her a present of Gregory's comparative view, inclosed
herewith, & that she will find in it a great deal of useful
advice for a young mother.   I hope herself & the child are
well.   kiss them both for me.   present me affectionately
to mrs Randolph & miss Jenny.   mend your Spanish
& your Harpsichord well and think often.   I always of

                                 Your's affectionately

P.S. letters inclosed with
the book for your sister.
                                 Th: Jefferson

On February 16, 1791, Jefferson replied to Maria's belated letter. "As
the spell is now broke" was Jefferson's way of encouraging Maria to
write more often. (Courtesy of the University of Virginia Library; photo
by Ed Roseberry.)

Anne, which I had recommended as belonging to both families. I wrote you in my last that the frogs had begun their songs on the 7th; since that the blue-birds saluted us on the 17th; the weeping-willow began to leaf on the 18th; the lilac and gooseberry on the 25th; and the golden-willow on the 26th. I inclose for your sister three kinds of flowering beans, very beautiful and very rare. She must plant and nourish them with her own hand this year, in order to save enough seeds for herself and me. Tell Mr. Randolph I have sold my tobacco for five dollars per c., and the rise between this and September. Warehouse and shipping expenses in Virginia, freight and storage here, come to 2s. 9d. a hundred, so that it is as if I had sold it in Richmond for 27s. 3d. credit till September, or half per cent. per month discount for the ready money. If he chooses it, his Bedford tobacco may be included in the sale. Kiss every body for me. Yours affectionately,

Th. Jefferson

Monticello, April 18th, 1791.

Dear Papa—I received your letter of March 31st the 14th of this month; as for that of March 9, I received it some time last month, but I do not remember the day. I have finished Don Quixote, and as I have not Desoles yet, I shall read Lazarillo de Tormes. The garden is backward, the inclosure having but lately been finished. I wish you would be so kind as to send me seven yards of cloth like the piece I send you. Adieu, my dear papa.

I am your affectionate daughter,
Maria Jefferson.

Philadelphia, April 24th, 1791.

I have received, my dear Maria, your letter of March 26th. I find I have counted too much on you as a Botanical and Zoological correspondent, for I undertook to affirm here that the fruit was not killed in Virginia, because I had a young daughter there who was in that kind of correspondence with me, and who, I was sure, would have mentioned it if it had been so. However, I shall go on communicating to you whatever may contribute to a comparative estimate of the two climates, in hopes it will induce you to do the same to me. Instead of waiting to send the two veils for your sister and yourself round with the other things, I inclose them with this letter. Observe that one of the strings is to be drawn tight round the root of the crown of the hat, and the veil then falling over the brim of the hat, is drawn by the lower string as tight or loose as you please round the neck. When the veil is not chosen to be down, the lower string is also tied round the root of the crown, so as to give the appearance of a puffed bandage for the hat. I send also inclosed the green lining for the calash. J. Eppes is arrived here. Present my affections to Mr. R., your sister, and niece.

Yours with tender love.
Th. Jefferson.

April 5.   Apricots in bloom.
           Cherry leafing.
  "   9.   Peach in bloom.
           Apple leafing.
  " 11.   Cherry in blossom.

Philadelphia, May 8th, 1791.

My Dear Maria,—Your letter of April 18th came to hand on the 30th; that of May 1st I received last night. By the stage which carries this letter I send you twelve yards of striped nankeen of the pattern inclosed. It is addressed to the care of Mr. Brown, merchant in Richmond, and will arrive there with this letter. There are no stuffs here of the kind you sent. April 30th the lilac blossomed. May 4th the gelder-rose, dogwood, redbud, azalea were in blossom. We have still pretty constant fires here. I shall answer Mr. Randolph's letter a week hence. It will be the last I shall write to Monticello for some weeks, because about this day se'nnight I set out to join Mr. Madison at New York, from whence we shall go up to Albany and Lake George, then cross over to Bennington, and so through Vermont to the Connecticut River, down Connecticut River, by Hartford, to New Haven, then to New York and Philadelphia. Take a map and trace this route. I expect to be back in Philadelphia about the middle of June. I am glad you are to learn to ride, but hope that your horse is very gentle, and that you will never be venturesome. A lady should never ride a horse which she might not safely ride without a bridle. I long to be with you all. Kiss the little one every morning for me, and learn her to run about before I come. Adieu, my dear. Yours affectionately.

My Dear Papa   May 29, 1791
I am much obliged to you for the veil that you sent me and shall allways were it I have begun to learn botany and arithmetic with mr Randolph the mare that he bought for me is come she is very pretty and is sister to Brimmer she can only trot and canter the fruit was not killed as you thought we have a great abundance of it here adieu Dear Papa I am your affectionate daughter. . . .

                                                Maria Jefferson

My dear Papa: Monticello, July 10th, 1791
I have received both your letters, that from Lake George and of June the 26th. I am much obliged to you for them and think the bark you wrote on prettier than paper. Mrs. Monroe and Aunt Bolling are here. My aunt would have written to you but she was unwell. She intends to go to the North Garden. Mr. Monroe is gone to Williamsburg to stay two or three weeks, and has left his lady here. She is a charming

woman. My sweet Anne grows prettier every day. I thank you for the pictures and nankeen that you sent me, which is I think very pretty. Adieu, dear papa

> I am your affectionate daughter
> Maria Jefferson

My Dear Maria: Philadelphia, August 21st, 1791. Your letter of July 10th is the last news I have from Monticello. The time of my setting out for that place is now fixed to some time in the first week of September, so that I hope to be there between the 10th and 15th. My horse is still in such a condition as to give little hope of his living: so that I expect to be under a necessity of buying one when I come to Virginia, as I informed Mr. Randolph in my last letter to him. I am in hopes, therefore, he will have fixed his eye on some one for me, if I should be obliged to buy. In the meantime, as Mr. Madison comes with me, he has a horse which will help us on to Virginia. Kiss little Anne for me and tell her to be putting on her best looks. My best affections to Mr. Randolph, your sister, and yourself. Adieu, my dear Maria.

> Th. Jefferson.

Jefferson's fall, 1791, vacation at Monticello lasted exactly a month, September 12 to October 12. The highlight of his stay was meeting his new granddaughter, Anne. His regret at curtailing his visit and resuming the cares of the State Department at Philadelphia was mitigated by the presence of Maria, who accompanied him. At the insistence of the First Lady, he and his lovely daughter stopped off at Mount Vernon, where Maria and Nelly Custis, Mrs. Washington's granddaughter, became such close friends that Maria was importuned to stay longer and ride in the coach-and-four when the President's entourage headed for Philadelphia, then the capital city. Meantime, Jefferson drove on to Philadelphia.

The Secretary of State's ménage at Philadelphia was now quite elaborate. He kept five horses, four or five salaried male servants as well as Maria's maid. And not to be overlooked was his cherished French chef, Petit, whose recent arrival was balm to Jefferson's heart and appetite.

On her arrival at Philadelphia, Maria was enrolled in Mrs. Pine's fashionable school at which, as Jefferson would later write Martha, "she has made young friends enough to keep herself in a bustle, and has been honored with visits of Mrs. Adams, Mrs. Randolph and Mrs. Rittenhouse. . . ."

For the next two years there were few letter-writing plaints to trouble Maria; her presence in Philadelphia solved that problem. She continued to attend Mrs. Pine's exclusive school though she managed to spend two or three days a week with her father lolling under the trees that shaded his house on the Schuylkill. She was "well and lazy"—as her father wrote Martha.

Maria had other interests, too, in Philadelphia. Her childhood playmate and future husband, Jack (John Wayles) Eppes of Eppington, was a freshman at college in Philadelphia. Under Jefferson's direction Jack was taking four hours of science and four of law each day. It would seem as if he took a good many other hours "consulting" Jefferson, most likely as an excuse to gaze on Maria's loveliness. Jack had never wavered in his devotion to her since she found her childhood home at Eppington when her father sailed away for Paris.

On January 5, 1794, Jefferson, having resigned his cabinet post, drove out of Philadelphia believing he would never again hold a major post in the federal government. Ten days later he reached Monticello to find his family assembled there to welcome him, including two small folk toddling about the mansion.

Maria, now fifteen, was a dazzling vision of beauty, though her loveliness was of such delicate cast that Abi-

On his return from France, in 1791, Jefferson accepted the post of Secretary of State. Maria—now a beautiful young girl of thirteen—attended Mrs. Pine's school and spent two or three days a week at her father's fine residence on the banks of the Schuylkill River in Philadelphia.

gail Adams was moved to write: "Slighter in person than her sister she already gave indications of superior beauty. It was that exquisite beauty possessed by her mother— that beauty which the experienced learn to look upon with dread, because it betrays a physical organization too delicately fine to withstand the rough shocks of the world."

Now—for the blessed three years of Jefferson's retreat from the political cockpit—Maria was again free of the dreaded letter-writing stint. But all too soon—for both— the time of respite ended. Jefferson would again find himself shouldering the burdens of political office—the vice-presidency; Maria would again find herself being chided for her letter-writing omissions.

"I have seen enough of political honors to know that they are but splendid torments"

In March, 1797, again facing years of separation from his beloved home and family, Jefferson was inaugurated as second Vice President of the still-youthful United States.

Then, in mid-June, Jefferson received a welcome letter: Martha had written the happy news that Maria had become engaged to her cousin, Jack Eppes. To Jefferson, it could hardly have been unexpected. Since his return from France, he had watched with interest—perhaps even tacitly encouraging—the young man's suit. Jack's affections had never wavered. His college days over, he was now a promising young lawyer. Jefferson avowed he could have searched the world over and not found anyone to whom he would rather entrust Maria's happiness than to Jack. Even at twenty-four the young man was already destined for politics. He would in time be elected to Congress, where his parliamentary skill would make him a leader of the Jefferson bloc in the House.

Jefferson promptly wrote Martha how happy her news had made him.

Philadelphia, June 8th, 1797.

I receive with inexpressible pleasure the information your letter contained. After your happy establishment, which has given me an inestimable friend, to whom I can leave the care of every thing I love, the only anxiety I had remaining was to see Maria also so associated as to insure her happiness. She could not have been more so to my wishes if I had had the whole earth free to have chosen a partner for her.

I now see our fireside formed into a group, no one member

of which has a fibre in their composition which can ever produce any jarring or jealousies among us. No irregular passions, no dangerous bias, which may render problematical the future fortunes and happiness of our descendants. We are quieted as to their condition for at least one generation more.

In order to keep us all together, instead of a present position in Bedford, as in your case, I think to open and resettle the plantation of Pantops for them. When I look to the ineffable pleasure of my family society, I become more and more disgusted with the jealousies, the hatred, and the rancorous and malignant passions of this scene, and lament my having ever again been drawn into public view. Tranquillity is now my object. I have seen enough of political honors to know that they are but splendid torments; and however one might be disposed to render services on which any of their fellow-citizens should set a value, yet, when as many would depreciate them as a public calamity, one may well entertain a modest doubt of their real importance, and feel the impulse of duty to be very weak. The real difficulty is, that being once delivered into the hands of others whose feelings are friendly to the individual and warm to the public cause, how to withdraw from them without leaving a dissatisfaction in their mind, and an impression of pusillanimity with the public.

On October 13, 1797, Maria Jefferson, 19, and John Wayles Eppes, 25, were married at Monticello. Tradition says she wore her mother's white satin bridal gown, but it is only a tradition. Jefferson urged the newly-weds to make their home at Monticello, but they settled, temporarily at least, at Eppington, which was as dear to Maria's heart as to Jack's. Her days of parental supervision were over— or were they?

In his first letter of the New Year, Jefferson could not resist offering Maria sage counsel about the marriage state into which she was so freshly embarked and the sources of discord between man and wife. He admitted he was sermonizing. After recommending strict economy in running her household because of the depressed state of agriculture and what it would mean to her planter-lawyer-husband, he cautioned her not to let economy interfere with pleasing her husband in the matter of dress.

Philadelphia, January 7th, '98.
I acknowledged, my dear Maria, the receipt of yours in a letter I wrote to Mr. Eppes. It gave me the welcome news that your sprain was well. But you are not to suppose it entirely so. The joint will remain weak for a considerable time, and give you occasional pains much longer. The state of things at * * * is truly distressing. Mr. * * * 's habitual intoxication will destroy himself, his fortune, and family. Of all calamities this is the greatest. I wish my sister could bear his misconduct with more patience. It would lessen his attachment to the bottle, and at any rate would make her own time more tolerable. When we see ourselves in a situation which must be endured and gone through, it is best to make up our minds to it, meet it with firmness, and accommodate everything to it in the best way practicable. This lessens the evil, while fretting and fuming only serves to increase our own torments. The errors and misfortunes of others should be a school for our own instruction. Harmony in the married state is the very first object to be aimed at. Nothing can preserve affections uninterrupted but a firm resolution never to differ in will, and a determination in each to consider the love of the other as of more value than any object whatever on which a wish had been fixed. How light, in fact, is the sacrifice of any other wish when weighed against the affections of one with whom we are to pass our whole life! And though opposition in a single instance will hardly of itself

produce alienation, yet every one has their pouch into which all these little oppositions are put; while that is filling the alienation is insensibly going on, and when filled it is complete. It would puzzle either to say why; because no one difference of opinion has been marked enough to produce a serious effect by itself. But he finds his affections wearied out by a constant stream of little checks and obstacles. Other sources of discontent, very common indeed, are the little cross-purposes of husband and wife, in common conversation, a disposition in either to criticise and question whatever the other says, a desire always to demonstrate and make him feel himself in the wrong, and especially in company. Nothing is so goading. Much better, therefore, if our companion views a thing in a light different from what we do, to leave him in quiet possession of his view. What is the use of rectifying him if the thing be unimportant; and if important, let it pass for the present, and wait a softer moment and more conciliatory occasion of revising the subject together. It is wonderful how many persons are rendered unhappy by inattention to these little rules of prudence.

I have been insensibly led, by the particular case you mention, to sermonize you on the subject generally; however, if it be the means of saving you from a single heartache, it will have contributed a great deal to my happiness; but before I finish the sermon, I must add a word on economy. The unprofitable condition of Virginia estates in general leaves it now next to impossible for the holder of one to avoid ruin. And this condition will continue until some change takes place in the mode of working them. In the mean time, nothing can save us and our children from beggary but a determination to get a year beforehand, and restrain ourselves vigorously this year to the clear profits of the last. If a debt is once contracted by a farmer, it is never paid but by a sale.

The article of dress is perhaps that in which economy is

the least to be recommended. It is so important to each to continue to please the other, that the happiness of both requires the most pointed attention to whatever may contribute to it—and the more as time makes greater inroads on our person. Yet, generally, we become slovenly in proportion as personal decay requires the contrary. I have great comfort in believing that your understanding and dispositions will engage your attention to these considerations; and that you are connected with a person and family, who of all within the circle of my acquaintance are most in the dispositions which will make you happy. Cultivate their affections, my dear, with assiduity. Think every sacrifice a gain which shall tend to attach them to you. My only object in life is to see yourself and your sister, and those deservedly dear to you, not only happy, but in no danger of becoming unhappy.

I have lately received a letter from your friend Kitty Church. I inclose it to you, and think the affectionate expressions relative to yourself, and the advances she has made, will require a letter from you to her. It will be impossible to get a crystal here to fit your watch without the watch itself. If you should know of any one coming to Philadelphia, send it to me, and I will get you a stock of crystals. The river being frozen up, I shall not be able to send you things till it opens, which will probably be some time·in February. I inclose to Mr. Eppes some pamphlets. Present me affectionately to all the family, and be assured of my tenderest love to yourself. Adieu.

Th. Jefferson.

But the delicate Maria was to have only six short years in which to practice her father's prudent counsels. By 1798, a dark thread began winding through his letters to his daughters: Maria's ill health. Jefferson's letters to Maria from 1798 to 1804 abound in expressions of his worry over her sicknesses and protestations of his love for her and pleas for her to "Nurse yourself, therefore, with all possible care for your own sake, for mine, and that of all those who love you" (July 13, 1798). News that Maria was "expecting" always filled Jefferson with dread. He was haunted by the specter of his wife's tragic experiences in childbirth and the little graves on the Monticello hillside.

On New Year's Day of 1799, Jefferson, now back in Philadelphia, welcomes in the New Year with a loving letter to Maria, in which he writes movingly:

However, when I am to write on politics I shall address my letter to Mr. Eppes. To you I had rather indulge the effusions of a heart which tenderly loves you, which builds its happiness on yours, and feels in every other object but little interest. Without an object here which is not alien to me, and barren of every delight, I turn to your situation with pleasure, in the midst of a good family which loves you, and merits all your love. Go on, my dear, in cultivating the invaluable possession of their affections. The circle of our nearest connections is the only one in which a faithful and lasting affection can be found, one which will adhere to us under all changes and chances. It is therefore the only soil on which it is worth while to bestow much culture. Of this truth you will become more convinced every day you advance into life.

A month later (on February 7, 1799) he is writing gratefully, on receipt of one of Maria's too-rare letters:

Your letter, my dear Maria, of January 21st, was received two days ago. It was, as Ossian says, or would say, like the bright beams of the moon on the desolate heath. Environed here in scenes of constant torment, malice and obloquy, worn down in a station where no effort to render service can avail anything, I feel not that existence is a blessing, but when something recalls my mind to my family or farm. This was the effect of your letter, and its affectionate expressions kindled up all those feelings of love for you and our dear connections which now constitute the only real happiness of my life.

Then, early in 1800, came the news of Maria's firstborn to delight Jefferson. In his exuberance over the new arrival he wrote a friend, "My daughter Eppes . . . lately presented me with the first honors of a grandfather on her part. Mrs. Randolph [Martha] has made them cease to be novelties—she has four children." To Catherine (Kitty) Church, Maria's dear friend at the Panthemont school in Paris, the proud grandfather promised a letter from Maria, though his scrupulous honesty forced him to add: "She was not much addicted to letter writing before [the event]; and I fear her new character of mother may furnish her new excuses for her remisses."

But the hold on life of Maria's youngling was too tenuous to last. Even before the new mother could get a congratulatory letter from her father, the feeble flame had flickered out and the desolate Maria had to bear the double burden of grief and a "long and painful convalescence." Like her beautiful, delicate mother, Maria was too fragile for childbearing.

Beautiful indeed were the opening lines of the letter Jefferson now wrote Maria, whose husband had conveyed the sad news to him:

Mr. Eppes's letter of January 17 had filled me with anxiety for your little one, and that of the 25th announced what I had feared. How deeply I feel it in all its bearings I shall not say—nor attempt consolation when I know that time and silence are the only medicines. I shall only observe, as a source of hope to us all, that you are young, and will not fail to possess enough of these dear pledges which bind us to one another and to life itself. (February 12, 1800.)

Later in the letter he went on to say:

It is necessary for my tranquillity that I should hear from you often; for I feel inexpressibly whatever affects your health or happiness. My attachments to the world, and whatever it can offer, are daily wearing off, but you are one of the links which hold to my existence, and can only break off with that. You have never, by a word or deed, given me one moment's uneasiness; on the contrary, I have felt perpetual gratitude to Heaven for having given me in you a source of so much pure and unmixed happiness; go on then, my dear, as you have done, in deserving the love of everybody; you will reap the rich reward of their esteem, and will find that we are working for ourselves while we do good to others.

On March 4, 1801, under clear, propitious skies, in the new capital Washington, Thomas Jefferson was sworn in as the third President of the United States, thus ending months of turmoil. The election campaign of the previous summer had been one of virulence and bitterness. Jefferson, the candidate of the newly formed Democratic-Republican party, had been attacked for almost everything he had ever said or done. He was an anarchist, a Bible-destroying infidel—so charged the Federalists. Taverns, courthouses, village greens, and drawing rooms everywhere rang with maledictions. Meanwhile, Jefferson waited out the storm at Monticello, tending his crops and speeding up the carpenters who were enlarging his home.

Then, early in January, the results of the election were revealed. President John Adams, a Federalist, had been defeated for the second term he sought; Jefferson had swept the popular vote, winning majorities in both

Houses of Congress; Jefferson and Aaron Burr (who had run on the Democratic-Republican ticket for Vice President) had each won seventy-three electoral votes. The House of Representatives, immured behind closed doors, settled down to break the tie between Jefferson and Burr for the presidency. Bitter partisan feeling gripped the nation's new permanent capital as did a prodigious snowstorm that blocked all avenues. Secession, even bloodshed, were in the air. On the day that Jefferson wrote the following letter to Maria, the third day of balloting, the House was bitterly deadlocked. Voting would continue two days more until the thirty-sixth ballot gave Jefferson the necessary votes of ten states, leaving the vice-presidency to Aaron Burr.

Washington, Feb. 15th, 1801.

Your letter, my dear Maria, of the 2d instant, came to hand on the 8th. I should have answered it immediately, according to our arrangement, but that I thought by waiting to the 11th I might possibly be able to communicate something on the subject of the election. However, after four days of balloting they are exactly where they were on the first. There is a strong expectation in some that they will coalesce tomorrow; but I know no foundation for it. Whatever event happens, I think I shall be at Monticello earlier than I formerly mentioned to you. I think it more likely I may be able to leave this place by the middle of March. I hope I shall find you at Monticello. The scene passing here makes me pant to be away from it; to fly from the circle of cabal, intrigue, and hatred, to one where all is love and peace. Though I never doubted of your affections, my dear, yet the expressions of them in your letter give me ineffable pleasure. No, never imagine that there can be a difference with me between yourself and your sister. You have both such dispositions as engross my whole love, and each so entirely that there can be

no greater degree of it than each possesses. Whatever absences I may be led into for a while, I look for happiness to
the moment when we can all be settled together no more to
separate. I feel a sincere wish indeed to see our Government
brought back to its republican principles, to see that kind of
government firmly fixed to which my whole life has been devoted. I hope we shall now see it so established, as that when
I retire it may be under full security, that we are to continue
free and happy. As soon as the fate of the election is over I
will drop a line to Mr. Eppes. I hope one of you will always
write the moment you receive a letter from me. Continue to
love me, my dear, as you ever have done, and ever have been
and will be by yours affectionately,

Th. Jefferson.

That summer of 1801, Maria was brought from Eppington to Monticello—where the newly inaugurated President awaited her arrival with impatience—with the horses
at a walk most of the way. Virginia roads were villainous,
and Maria was nearing her "time" again. But Jefferson
was denied the satisfaction of being on hand for the ac-
couchement; inexorable presidential duties called him
back to Washington late in September.

The autumn of 1801 was in full color when Maria's
second child was born at Monticello and promptly named
Francis Eppes. For weeks the health of mother and child
was precarious, and Jefferson, at Washington, was frantic
with anxiety.

In December, 1801, already burdened with the onerous
cares of his new high office, he wrote:

I perceive that it will be merely accidental when I can steal a
moment to write to you; however, that is of no consequence,
my health being always so firm as to leave you without doubt
on that subject. But it is not so with yourself and little one. I

shall not be easy, therefore, if either yourself or Mr. Eppes do not, once a week or fortnight, write the three words "all are well." That you may be so now, and so continue, is the subject of my perpetual anxiety, as my affections are constantly brooding over you. Heaven bless you, my dear daughter. Present me affectionately to Mr. Eppes and my friends at Eppington if you are there. (December 14, 1801.)

In the winter of 1802-1803, Maria's health had rallied enough for her to be able to fulfill a wish dear to her father's heart—that she and Martha visit him in the President's mansion at Washington. The visit was an unqualified success. For his beloved daughters, he broke out his rarest wines. Petit, his *maître d'hôtel,* dreamed up dishes of culinary art to please their palates. Guided by Dolley Madison, Maria and Martha canvassed the stylish shops to array themselves in the height of fashion.

On hand to greet them also were the two husbands, Thomas Mann Randolph and Jack Eppes, who had both won seats in the House of Representatives at the last election; they, too, were now also a source of pride to their father-in-law.

The proud father was transported as he watched the two young ladies carry Washington by storm. Diplomats, statesmen, dignitaries, and high government officials showered attentions on them, as they attended the rounds of balls, parties, dinners, and routs. Maria's rare beauty created a sensation. Martha's conversational talents and her brilliant intellect, so like her father's, charmed all she met.

"I have lost even the half of all I had"

The year 1804 found Jefferson at the high noon of his political career. The nation was at peace and prosperous. Jefferson's popularity was soaring. His first term as chief magistrate of the nation was ending in a blaze of glory. John Randolph of Roanoke put it succinctly: "Never was there an administration more brilliant than that of Mr. Jefferson up to this period. We were indeed in the 'full tide of successful experiment.' Taxes repealed; the public debt amply provided for, both interest and principal; sinecures abolished; Louisiana acquired; public confidence unbounded."

Yet Jefferson's enjoyment of his triumph was short-lived. Here, at the zenith of his public life, bitter personal tragedy struck him a merciless blow.

His "ever dear daughter Maria," who was spending the winter at Edgehill with her sister, was approaching her third confinement and was gravely ill. Martha herself had only recently increased her family with a "new bantling," as Jefferson called it, her sixth. Both husbands, Thomas Mann Randolph, Jr., and Jack Eppes were about to embark for the "lame duck" session of Congress soon to convene. "Terrible anxiety" gripped the President. He longed to hasten to Maria's side only to be enchained by the duty of waiting for Congress to "rise," probably the second week of March.

Separated from her husband, "the best beloved of my soul," waiting for a baby whose arrival was miscalculated, Maria found the going hard. With her frail, almost transparent hand she wrote her husband the last letter of her life, "Do not be uneasy my dearest husband. . . . The hope that in a week or two I shall be able to give you the intelligence most interesting and most desired, makes me support it with patience; to present you when we meet with so sweet an addition to our felicity would more than compensate for allmost any suffering."

From the President's mansion came loving, solicitous, encouraging letters. "Take care of yourself, my dearest Maria"—he exhorts (November 27, 1803)—"have good spirits, and know that courage is as essential to triumph in your case as in that of a soldier."

The day after Christmas, December 26, 1803, he is writing: "Not knowing the time destined for your expected indisposition, I am anxious on your account. You are prepared to meet it with courage, I hope. Some female friend of your mamma's (I forget whom) used to say it was no more than a jog of the elbow."

Jefferson must have used the old phrase to bolster his sinking heart. For in the same letter, he urges that "The material thing is, to have scientific aid in readiness, that if anything uncommon takes place it may be redressed on the spot, and not be made serious by delay. It is a case which least of all will wait for doctors to be sent for, therefore with the single precaution nothing is ever to be feared. I was in hopes to have heard from Edgehill last night, but I suppose your post has failed." Jefferson doesn't make clear what he considered scientific aid—in this era, delivering babies was in the hands of unskilled doctors, midwives, journeying medicine men, and members of the family.

In mid-February, 1804, Maria's "sweet addition" arrived, to be immediately named Maria for her mother whose protracted struggle had left her weakened and exhausted. At the time, Jack Eppes was in Washington. The news reached Jefferson on February 26. His fears were somewhat allayed and his spirits rose. Maria could now convalesce. He wrote at once congratulating his daughter with "a thousand joys" on the "happy accession to your family." Only the previous day the Republican congressional caucus had endorsed him for a second presidential term, which was tantamount to reelection. But political honors were no balm to his heart at this moment.

Washington, Feb. 26th, 1804.

A thousand joys to you, my dear Maria, on the happy accession to your family. A letter from our dear Martha by last post gave me the happy news that your crisis was happily over, and all well. I had supposed that if you were a little later than your calculation, and the rising of Congress as early as we expected, we might have been with you at the moment when it would have been so encouraging to have had your friends around you. I rejoice, indeed, that all is so well.

Congress talk of rising the 12th of March; but they will probably be some days later. You will doubtless see Mr. Eppes and Mr. Randolph immediately on the rising of Congress. I shall hardly be able to get away till some days after them. By that time I hope you will be able to go with us to Monticello, and that we shall *all* be there together for a month; and the interval between that and the autumnal visit will not be long. Will you desire your sister to send for Mr. Lilly, and to advise him what orders to give Goliath for providing those vegetables which may come into use for the months of April, August, and September? Deliver her also my affectionate love. I will write to her the next week. Kiss all the little ones, and be assured yourself of my tender and unchangeable affection.

Th. Jefferson.

Five days later his heart sank again. Maria's condition was critical. Jack Eppes left at once for Edgehill and his wife's side. A three days' journey then, instead of three hours as nowadays. Jefferson wrote Maria at once. It was almost his last letter to her.

Washington, Mar. 3d, 1804.

The account of your illness, my dearest Maria, was known to me only this morning. Nothing but the impossibility of Congress proceeding a single step in my absence presents an insuperable bar. Mr. Eppes goes off, and I hope will find you in a convalescent state. Next to the desire that it may be so, is that of being speedily informed, and of being relieved from the terrible anxiety in which I shall be till I hear from you. God bless you, my ever dear daughter, and preserve you safe to the blessing of us all.

Th. Jefferson.

On March 8 a note from Martha gave Jefferson's hopes a lift. To it, he replied:

Washington Mar. 8. 04.

Your letter of the 7th my dear Martha, which was not received till the last night has raised me to life again—for four days past I had gone through inexpressible anxiety, the mail which left you on the 5th. will probably be here tonight, and will I hope strengthen our hopes of Maria's continuing to recover, and mr. Eppes's arrival which I presume was on the 6th. will render her spirits triumphant over her physical debility. Congress have determined to rise on Monday sennight (the 19th.) your Randolph will probably be with you on the 22d. and myself within 3 or 4 days after. Maria must in the meantime resolve to get strong to make us all happy. Your apologies my dear for using any thing at Monticello for her, yourself, family or friends, are more than unnecessary. What is there is as much for the use of you all as for myself, and you cannot do me greater pleasure than by using every thing with the same freedom I should do myself. tell my dear Maria to be of good cheer, and to be ready to mount on horseback with us and continue to let us hear of her by every post. if mrs Lewis be still with you deliver her my affectionate respects and assurances of my great sensibility for her kind attentions to Maria. kiss the little ones for me, and be assured of my tenderest love to Maria & yourself.

Th. Jefferson

Meanwhile, Jack Eppes had arrived and found Maria a trifle improved and so reported at once to the anxious father. Jefferson answered hopefully, advising for Maria a diet of "light food and cordial wine." He said, "The sherry at Monticello is old and genuine, and the Pedro Ximines older still and stomachic."

On March 27, Congress rose and Jefferson hurried homeward. Spring was bursting over the mountain when he drove up to Edgehill on April 5 to find Maria in a shocking state of debility and fading fast. Today she was better, tomorrow worse. So it went. Panic-stricken, he had four slaves carry her on a litter the four miles to Monticello. Change of place, the air and sunshine around Monticello, might restore her. So he reasoned in his distress. On soft, sunny days they rolled her out across the glistening green lawn, but to no avail. The little mountain was arrayed in the first blooms of spring when, on April 17, she died. She was almost twenty-six.

Once again Jefferson turned to the page of his prayer book where he had entered the date of her birth in 1778. To it he now added the brief closing saga of her life, "Died April 17, 1804, between 8 and 9 A.M." Too soon the infant Maria would follow her mother to a tiny grave on the slopes of Monticello.

In reply to a letter of condolence from his old and constant friend, Governor John Page of Virginia, Jefferson wrote plaintively, "Others may lose of their abundance, but I, of my want, have lost even the half of all I have. My evening prospects now hang on the slender thread of a single life."

I I I

Ellen Wayles Randolph

1 7 9 6 - 1 8 7 6

"I have given this letter 20 kisses . . .
half to yourself, the other half you
must give to Anne"

On a warm July morning in 1802, Miss Ellen Randolph
of Edgehill, Virginia, aged six, received this exciting note
from her grandfather, the President of the United States:

My very dear Ellen
I will catch you in bed Sunday or Monday morning.
> Yours affectionately,
> Th: Jefferson

It is not on record whether the President caught "Miss
Eleanor" abed when he reached Monticello early Sunday
morning, July 25. His threat of surprising her in the early

hours of the morning was a playful custom of his. More than likely the forehanded little lady was up betimes that Sunday morning, waiting on the east veranda to greet him with a kiss when his chaise crunched to a stop.

Ellen Wayles Randolph was born in 1796, third child of Jefferson's older daughter, Martha Jefferson Randolph. Jefferson was elected Vice President that same year. Of his many granddaughters she was his favorite, his playmate. To her he wrote more letters than to any of the other five, though he loved them all. This delightful correspondence with her distinguished grandsire began in 1801, when Ellen was five. Her letters to him and his to her (most of them unpublished up to now) have lost none of their quaint charm though hidden away for a century and a quarter.

The interchange of letters between Ellen and the President continued on through her childhood to the end of his second term in 1809, though it can be said truly that the correspondence ran on for twenty-five years until shortly before his death in 1826. At times during his Washington residency he had to coax letters out of her. Often hers outnumbered his. But the correspondence was quite extensive. She was as persevering as a very young lady could be in mastering the goose-quill art. Like her grandfather she was, it seems, an indefatigable letterwriter once she got started.

In his letters to Ellen, Jefferson often enclosed "pieces" for her scrapbook, which was his favorite way of fostering his grandchildren's interest in things of the mind. He required each of them to keep a scrapbook, a sort of literary garden, in which they pasted poems, bright sayings, extracts from books suitable to their ages that he clipped from newspapers and sent on to them.

Ellen repaid her grandfather's devotion to her with enduring love. In later years she said she gave him "all the affection and something of the loyalty of a subject."

When in 1809, Jefferson retired to Monticello, Ellen's

association with him became even closer. That same year her mother, Martha Randolph, moved her still-increasing brood of Randolphs from Edgehill to Monticello, so that she could preside over her father's establishment soon to become a mecca for swarms of visitors drawn to the magic mountain from all ranks of life.

Ellen's first letter to her grandfather was written for her by her mother after his return to Washington in the fall of 1801 from his "summer capital" (Monticello). Jefferson answered it as though she had written it herself, addressing it quite formally to "Miss Eleanor Randolph." In jest, of course, he complimented her on learning to read and write so quickly; when he had left Monticello on September 27, five-year-old Ellen could do neither.

My dear Ellen,   Washington November 27, 1801
I have received your letter and am very happy to learn you have made such rapid progress in learning. When I left Monticello you could not read and now I find you can not only read but write also. I inclose you two little books as a mark of satisfaction, and if you continue to learn as fast you will become a learned lady and publish books yourself. I hope you will at the same time continue to be a very good girl, never getting angry with your playmates nor the servants, but always trying to be more good humored and more generous than they. If you find that one of them has been better tempered to you than you to them, you must blush, and be very much ashamed, and resolve not to let them excel you again. In this way you will make us all too fond of you, and I shall particularly think of nothing but what I can send you or carry you to show you how much I love you. . . . I have given this letter 20 kisses which it will deliver to you: half to yourself, and the other half you must give to Anne [Ellen's older sister]. Adieu my dear Ellen.

                                        Th. Jefferson

Thomas Jefferson
President of the U. S.

Washington

Here is one of the many envelopes Ellen addressed to her grandfather,
the President of the United States. (*Courtesy of the Massachusetts Historical Society.*)

The President's letter had more influence than he had
perhaps considered. Ellen's mother conceded that "if
they [her children] turn out well with regard to morals
I *ought* to be satisfied, though I *feel* that I never can sit
down quietly under the idea of their being blockheads"
(April 16, 1802). So she was delighted to report in that
letter:

Ellen reads, not very correctly it is true, but in a way speedily to do so, I hope. For which I really think we are indebted to your letter expressing your surprise at her having
in so short a time learned to read and write; she began with
it herself, and by continually spelling out lines, putting
them together, and then reading them to whoever would lis-
ten to her, she convinced me of the practicability of carrying
on reading and spelling together, before, in the regular

course of business, she had got into two syllables. The writing she attempted also but the trouble was so much greater than any end to be attained . . . to defer that part of her education to a more distant one. (April 16, 1802.)

> Ellen's first extant letter to her grandfather, written in her own big round hand, is dated February 22, 1805. She was now eight, but her mother ruled the paper with delicate lines and helped her with the spelling.

My dear GrandPapa   February 22, 1805
I received your letter and am very much obliged to you for it, as it is very seldom that I get one you cannot think how glad I was at it. I am very much obliged to you for the bantams you promised me and will take great care of them. I go on very slowly with my French for I have got through but one book of Telemachus but I hope that I shall now go on better since Mamma's health is so much better that she is able to hear us our lessons regularly. Give my love to Papa and Mrs. H. Smith [a family friend]. Adieu my Dear GrandPapa believe me to be your affectionate GrandDaughter
                              Ellen Wayles Randolph

> Jefferson replied on March 4, 1805, the day of his second inauguration as President. He found time even amid the gala festivities and "pressure" of that great day to indite a charming letter to Ellen and to enclose a poem and several other "pieces" for her scrapbook. He neglected to say that he had that morning mounted his favorite horse, Wildair, and led the first inaugural parade from the Capitol down Pennsylvania Avenue and on past the President's mansion.

My dearest Ellen,   Washington, Mar. 4, '05
I owe a letter to you & one to your sister Anne. but the pres-

sure of the day on which this is written, and your Papa's departure permits me to write only to you, to inclose you a poem about another namesake of yours, and some other pieces worth preserving. as I expect Anne's volume is now large enough, I will begin to furnish you with materials for one—I know you have been collecting some yourself; but as I expect there is some tag, rag & bobtail verse among it you must begin a new volume for my materials. I am called off by company therefore God bless you, my dear child, kiss your Mama and sisters for me, & tell them I shall be with them in about a week from this time. Once more adieu.

Th. Jefferson.

President Jefferson paused amid the "pressure" of the day of his second inauguration, March 4, 1805, to write a few lines to Ellen, then nine, and send her several bits of poetry for her scrapbook. (Courtesy of the Massachusetts Historical Society.)

My dearest Ellen   *Washington Mar. 4. 05.*

Late in the spring of 1805, "Miss Eleanor Randolph" received from her grandfather an amusing statement of her delinquent correspondence account, to which he attached a letter asking her to put on her "boots & spurs" and ride over to Monticello and report to him on his shrubbery. He also threatened to send the sheriff after her unless she "paid" her letter-bill. (It was about four miles round-about from the Randolph home, Edgehill, to Monticello.)

Miss Eleanor W. Randolph to Th. Jefferson   Dr

1805 May 21	To a letter which ought to be written once in every three weeks while I am here, to wit from Jan. 1, 1805, to this day, 15 weeks	5.
	Cr	
Feb. 23	By one single letter of this day's date	1.
	Balance due from E. W. Randolph to Th. J.	4.
		5

So stands the account for this year, my dear Ellen, between you and me. Unless it be soon paid off I shall send the sheriff after you. I inclose you an abundant supply of poetry, among which you will find Goody Blake, which I think you wanted. I will thank you if you will put on your boots & spurs & ride to Monticello and inform me how my thorns live. This part of the country is beautifying with them so fast that every ride I take makes me anxious for those at Monticello. Your Papa in his last letter informs me the mumps have got into the family. Let me know who have it and how all do. Kiss your dear Mamma for me & shake hands with all the little ones. Present me affectionately to your Papa & accept *mes baise-mains* yourself.

Th. Jefferson

Not until June did Ellen muster up enough what-it-takes to reply to her grandfather's threat. She was probably a bit appalled by the idea of corresponding with the President of the United States, even though he was her grandfather.

Dear Grand Papa   [Rec'd June 27.05]
I now set down to write to you and hope you will answer my letter I have often tried to do it before but never could succeed, but now I am determined to do it. I suppose you have heard that Cousin Eliza Pleasants is gone away. Uncle William and Mr Hackley have been here and left us yesterday esccuse the faults and bad writing of this letter since [nothing] but [my] ansciety to write to you and to show you I have not forgotten you could have [made] me do it your affectionate Grand Daughter

Elleonora W Randolph

July 10, 1805, found Jefferson writing Ellen a letter one would hardly expect him to write to a child of eight. Her missive that inspired his answer is unfortunately lost, though apparently she wrote to ask: What are the fine arts? How many are there? Enormously pleased that his granddaughter should evince an interest in such things at her age, Jefferson answered her seriously.

My dearest Ellen,   Washington July 10.05
To answer the question in your letter of the 4th I must observe that neither the *number* of the fine arts nor the particular arts entitled to that appellation have been fixed by general consent. many reckon but five. Painting, sculpture, architecture, music & poetry. to these some have added Oratory, including within that Rhetoric which is the art of style & composition. Others again, add gardening as a 7th fine art. not horticulture, but the art of embellishing grounds by

Dear Grand Papa

I now set down to write to
you and hope you will answer
my letter I have often tried to
do it before but never could
succeed, but now I am determined
to do it I suppose you have heard
that cousin Eliza Pleasants
is gone away Uncle William
and Mr Hackley have been
here and left us yesterday

excuse the faults and bad writing
of this letter since nothing but my anxiety
to write to you and to show you I have
not forgotten you could have made me do it
your affectionate Grand Daughter
Elleonora W Randolph

In her letter to her beloved "Grand Papa," which Jefferson received on June 27, 1805, Ellen included some of the "news from home" that Jefferson longed to hear. The brief note was written "to show you I have not forgotten you." (Courtesy of the Massachusetts Historical Society.)

fancy. I think L. Kaims has justly proved this to be entitled to the appellation of a fine art. It is nearly allied to landscape painting & accordingly we generally find the landscape painter the best designer of a garden. no perfect *definition* of what is a fine art has ever yet been given. some say that as those are *mechanical* arts which consist in manual operation unconnected with the understanding, those are *fine* arts which to manual operation join the exercise of the imagination or genius. This would comprehend sculpture, painting, architecture & gardening, but neither, poetry, nor oratory. Others say that the sciences are objects of the understanding, the fine arts of the senses. This would add gardening, but neither poetry nor oratory. a definition which should include Poetry & Oratory & no more would be very difficult to form. I have delivered your love to mrs Smith. I will bring mine to you all on Thursday, Friday or Saturday next. the thermometer was yesterday at 97½° here, and at 96° the two preceding days. I think it will be at 98° to-day. should it be as hot when I am ready to depart, I shall certainly delay my departure. God bless you all.

Th: Jefferson

Jefferson's disquisition on the fine arts took its time reaching Monticello so the young miss, anxious for answers to her questions, wrote again, though neglecting to date her letter. She voiced disappointment that the President had not answered her inquiries and said so plainly. She was rewarded shortly when the "post" brought his reply.

How was I disappointed at not receiving a letter from my dear GrandPapa this Post in answer to one I wrote him! You said in your last letter to Sister Anne that you expected but a short one from me, however I am determined to keep up a regular correspondence, if possible. You said also that you would catch me in bed the morning of the 18, 19, or 20 of this week; I hope you will not, for I shall rise betimes all three mornings I expect you. Aunt has had the mumps and is not quite recovered. I am very much obliged to you for the Poetry you sent me and think it all very Pretty, particularly *Little John* and the *Ode to Modesty.* Sister Anne's fowls are increased greatly. My hen has laid a great many eggs not fit for hatching. Adieu my dear Grand Papa believe me to be your affectionate GrandDaughter

E. W. Randolph

Hereabouts Ellen's letters begin to reveal the rapid development of her inquiring mind. She was putting aside childish ways. She was, so she said in this next letter, determined to keep up a "regular correspondence" with her grandfather.

Dear Grand Papa, November 10, 1805.
I expect you think I have forgotten the Promise I made you of writing to you every Post but I have not for I have tried several times but could not effect it for want of impliments to do it. You must answer my letter for it would give me great Pleasure to keep up a regular Correspondence with you. I have no news to tell you except the report that prevails that of Mrs. Trists marriage with Governor Claiborne. I suppose you have heard it. It is time to finish my letter I have written enough for this time. Sister Anne gives her love to you and says she will write to you shortly. Mamma gives hers to you also as do all the children. Give mine to Mrs. Smith and tell her I hope I shall see her soon. Adieu my Dear Grand Papa believe me to be your affectionate Grand Daughter, Ellen Wayles Randolph, Edgehill.

My dearest Ellen Washington, Nov. 24, '05
Your letter of the 10th did not get here till the 19th and this

is the first post-day since that for answering it. . . . It is expected that Mrs. Madison will leave Philadelphia tomorrow and be here with Mrs. Cutts in the course of the week. She will of course be here before you. I believe I formerly inclosed the poem now sent; but not being certain & its merit considerable I now forward it. In hopes of soon seeing you I shall only add kisses for your Mamma & sisters & yourself, and my affectionate salutations to your Papa.

Th. Jefferson

Jefferson's foregoing letter to Ellen gave the Randolph children a huge thrill. The long-awaited trip to Washington to visit the President was just around the corner. Ellen's mother, Martha, was "expecting" any moment but that was no reason to postpone the visit to grandfather's. By now Martha was adept at child bearing.

Very soon they were all squeezed into a big carryall with four horses out front and went lurching off to the capital where they spent the winter in the Executive Mansion, which Jefferson once described as a "great stone house, big enough for two emperors, one pope and the grand lama into the bargain." While there Martha Randolph made history by presenting the President with another grandson, the first baby born in the President's Mansion. He promptly named the newcomer after his old friend, James Madison. During her visit Ellen was delighted to renew her friendship with Mrs. Harrison Smith (nee Margaret Bayard), the family friend she had met as a very little girl on her previous visit. Of Ellen, Mrs. Smith later wrote, "She is singularly and extravagantly fond of poetry . . . without exception one of the finest and most intelligent children I have ever met with." Ellen's love of poetry was no doubt inspired by poems Jefferson sent her for her scrapbook.

Soon after the Randolphs returned to Virginia, Jefferson was writing in concern:

One of the most famous of the Jefferson portraits is this one, painted by Rembrandt Peale, son of his old friend Charles Willson Peale. Jefferson sat for this in January, 1805, at the President's Mansion, Washington. (Courtesy of the New York Historical Society.)

Washington June 24.06.
I learn with deep concern, my dearest Ellen, that the family
has been unwell generally, that you have been ill, and your
Mama indisposed. Anne informs me you are getting better
but does not say whether your Mama is so also. Yet, in the
absence of your Papa, her health is doubly important because her care is necessary for you all. I hope this will find
you all recovered. Your friends here are generally well. Mrs.
S. H. Smith remains constantly in the country, and this place
is duller than I ever saw it. I certainly have never been so
tired of it; yet I do not at present expect to leave it till the
21st. of July, and on the 24th shall expect to catch you in bed,
and to be happy in the midst of you. in the meantime God
bless you all, and have you and your precious Mama in his
holykeeping. give her my tenderest kisses, & to all the little
ones; to your Papa, if returned my sincere affections.

Th. Jefferson

My dearest Ellen   Washington Nov. 30.06.
I have recieved two letters from you since I left Monticello,
by Davy I sent you a pair of Bantam fowls; quite young: so
that I am in hopes you will now be enabled to raise some. I
propose on their subject a question of natural history for your
enquiry: that is whether this is the Gallina Adrianisa, or
Adria, the Adriatick cock of Aristotle? for this you must examine Buffon, etc. Mr. Burwell asked in the name of your
Mama, for a Nautical almanac. She will find those of many
years in the library at Monticello, in the press on the right
hand of the Eastern outward door of the cabinet. I send you
inclosed much newspaper poetry. Adieu my dear Ellen: kiss
your mama for me and all the young ones. for yourself recieve the kiss I give to this paper.

Th: Jefferson

Dear Grandpapa   Edgehill December 12th 1806
I recieved the Bantams for which I am very much obliged
to you they seem to be larger, and younger, than the first and
I think them handsomer. I have no news to tell you for being in the country I seldom have any thing worth relating
and that being the case I can never write long letters unless
you suffer me to speak of myself. I have begun the Grecian
History in which I am very much interested and have got to
multiplication in arithmetic. I am going on with Dufief and
am reading Plutarque de la [. . .] in French of which I read
ten pages for my lesson sometimes more but not often less. I
copy the historical part of Lord Chesterfield's letters for a
lesson in writing, all which is generally concluded by dinner
time after which I play and at night sew while Sister Ann
reads aloud to us. adieu my Dear Grand Papa. Mama and
the children join in love to you believe me to be your affectionate Grand Daughter E. W. R.

Mama says Buffon cannot answer the question you propose to me.

My dearest Ellen   Washington Dec. 15.06
This is our postday, and I have been so engaged that the
hour of dinner & company are arriving before I could begin
a letter to you. I shall therefore merely say we are all well, &
I hope we shall hear to-night that all are well at Edgehill.
Tell your Mama, while you kiss her for me, that Rigdon has
returned & delivered me her watch neatly done which will
be sent by your papa. I send you something for your collection. Kiss & bless all the young people for me, and be assured
of my affectionate love.

Th. Jefferson

Edgehill December 27th 1806
I could not miss so good an opportunity of writing to you my

Dear Grand Papa as now offers itself to tell you I do not regard your not punctually answering my letters as I know how many you have to write. your grass still continues to look very well and will I hope all the winter. I rely upon your indulgence to excuse this short letter as I have not any thing to say to you Mama, Sister Ann, and the children send their love to you give mine to Mrs. S. H. Smith adieu my Dear Grandpapa believe me to be your affectionate Grand Daughter E. W. Randolph.

Edgehill January 30th 1807

It has been a long time since I have heard from my Dear Grandpapa although he is two letters in my debt one of which I expected last post but not recieving it I concluded it would be better to set down and write to put you in mind of your promise of writing to me sometimes. Jefferson [Ellen's older brother, Thomas Jefferson Randolph] has returned and so has Mr. Ogilvie who is going to be married to Mrs. Bankhead of Port Royal who is the widow of a gentleman who had been his pupil. she is (I am informed) a fine woman and very rich. besides she is rather handsome than otherwise Mr. O. intends to settle with her in Milton it will a great addition to our neighbourhood. James [Ellen's baby brother, James Madison Randolph] is very much grown and I think now is a very handsome and sprightly child Mama Sister Ann and the children are well and send their love to you give mine to Mrs. S. H. S. adieu my dear Grandpapa, believe me to be your affectionate Grand Daughter E. W. Randolph

Your grass looks very well.

On February 8, 1807, Jefferson wrote one of the most amusing letters of this long correspondence. In it he displayed a very human characteristic: his yearning for small

news of the homefolks. Ellen sought to gratify him. Her
letters became more numerous, and she filled them with
things he wanted to hear: small news of Monticello and
the wee ones at Edgehill and chitchat of the neighborhood—appealing tidbits that must have warmed Jefferson's heart.

My dearest Ellen,   Washington, Feb. 8, '07.
I believe it is true that you have written me 2 letters to
my one to you. Whether this proceeds from you having more
industry or less to do than myself I will not say. One thing
however I will say that I most sincerely wish to be with you
all, and settle the point *viva voce* (if you do not understand
these two Latin words you must lay Jefferson's Latin under
contribution that you may know because they are often used
in English writing). To return to our correspondence, you
have a great advantage as to matter for communication. You
have a thousand little things which I am fond to hear; for
instance the health of everybody . . . then what you are
reading, what are your other occupations, how many dozen
bantams you have raised, how often you and Anne have
rode to Monticello to see if the tulips are safe etc. etc. etc.
However I shall be with you about the 11th or 12th *proxim*
(more Latin, madam) and then we will examine the tulips
together. Kiss your dear Mamma a thousand times for me,
and all the sisters *q.s.* (more Latin) and be assured yourself
of my tender affections.

Th. Jefferson

Dear Grand Papa   Feb. 14 1807
I suspect that it would be more reasonable to think that your
owing me 3 letters proceeds from my having more time than
industry although a very little part of this winter has been
spent by me in Idleness still however I think that you must

have a great deal more to do than I have. Mama has been un-well for several days but I hope she will soon recover all the children are in good health as for the Bantam she laid one egg in the cold weather and eat it up I am very much afraid she will so all the others so if she does she will be as worth-less as the others but in spite of that I am very fond of them and think them very handsome the old ones are quite tame but the new much to the contrary. I have not finished the Grecian history but I shall very soon. I have read in French the first volume of Plutarque de La [. . .] which contains almost entirely Grecian Lives I do not intend to read the lives of the modern great men yet. I have advanced but slowly in my arithmetic but the reason was that Mama wished me to be perfect in one rule before I went into an-other. Your grass looks very well but I am afraid your wall-flower is dead. Mama Sister Ann and the children send their love to you give mine to Mrs. S. H. Smith. adieu my Dear Grandpapa believe me to be your most affectionate Grand Daughter.

E. W. Randolph.

My dearest Ellen   Washington Mar. 1.07.
I am afraid I shall be bankrupt in my epistolary account with Anne & yourself. however the tide of business, like that of the ocean, will wait for nobody. I send for Cornelia a lit-tle poem, the grasshopper's ball, to begin her collection. The Yankee story is for yourself. Thank Mary for her letter, but tell her it is written in a cypher of which I have not the key, she must therefore tell it all to me when I come home. I shall write to Anne by the cart, because it will carry a box of flower roots which I shall consign to her care, but not to be opened till we get to Monticello, & have every thing ready for planting them as soon as they are opened. I shall write by

this post to your Mama, so I conclude with my kisses to you all.

Th. Jefferson

Dear Grandpapa Edgehill March 6th 1807
Your fear of being a bankrupt is not badly founded for I think if we were to count our letters you would owe me a great many I do, not however desire that you should pay me all as you have already too many to write I only wish that you should keep up the correspondence by writing some-times to me. Cornelia is very much pleased with the piece of poetry you sent her. Mary says she would tell you what was in her letter gladly if she knew herself. your grass looks very well and when you come you will see it is quite green and handsome. Sister Ann and the children send their loves to you give mine to Mrs. S. H. Smith when next you see her adieu my Dear Grandpapa believe me to be your most affectionate Grand Daughter.

E. W. Randolph

My dear Ellen Washington June 29.07.
I believe I have recieved no letter from you since I came from Monticello, but perhaps there is one on the road for me. hope is so much pleasanter than despair, that I always prefer looking into futurity through her glass. I send you some poetical gleanings. our newspapers have been rather barren in that ware for some time past. Whether the muses have been taking a nap, or our news writers have been pre-vented from making their weekly visits to mount Parnassus, by their occupations with Burr & the Chesapeake I cannot decide. but we will leave these idle ladies to their dreams in the Castalian valley, & descend to the more useful region & occupations of the good housewife, one of whom is worth

more than the whole family of the muses. How go on the Bantams? I rely on you for their care, as I do on Anne for the Algerine fowls, & on our arrangements at Monticello for the East Indians. These varieties are pleasant for the table & furnish an agreeable diversification in our domestic occupations. I am now possessed of individuals of four of the most remarkeable varieties of the race of the sheep. if you turn to your books of natural history, you will find among these 1. the Spanish sheep or Marino. 2. the Iceland sheep, or Ovis Polycerata. 3. The Barbary sheep, or Ovis laticauda & 4. the Senegal sheep, or that of Bengal which is the same. I have lately recieved a ram of the 2d kind, who has 4 horns, a round & beautiful animal, rather small. the 3d or broadtailed is remarkable for its flavor. I lately had a quarter sent me which I found the highest flavored lamb I had ever tasted. The 4th. or Senegal is supposed to be the original stock of the sheep. it's flavor is said to be equal to that of venison. tho' I possess individuals of one sex only of the 2d, 3d, & 4th kinds, yet a crossings are understood by naturalists to produce the true breed. I mean to pay great attention to them, pro bono publico. (call on Jefferson to translate your Latin) tell your Papa the only true account of the affair of the Chesapeake is that in Smith's paper. the others are full of falsehoods. present my warm affections to your Papa, Mama & the young ones, & be assured of a full share of them yourself.

Th. Jefferson

Jefferson came home in early August, 1807, for his summer vacation. Not until November after his return to Washington did Ellen renew her correspondence with him.

Edgehill November 11th 1807
This is the second letter I have written to my dear grandpapa

without recieving an answer but as I know the reason I will continue to write untill you have leisure to answer my letters. one of my poor little Bantams is dead and the one which I liked best although it was the old one he had got so tame that he would fly up in my lap and eat out of my hand all the children were sorry at his death. Cousin Polly Harrison was in the neighbourhood lately and has left Jane to stay with me untill the exibition which is to commence Wednesday the 11th and will finish saturday when there will be a ball to which we are all going. I have only two dances to go to before the school will be broken up for which I will be sorry Aunt Virginia has not quitted us yet but expects to go down soon Mama Aunt Virginia Sister Ann and all the children send their love to you give mine to Mrs. S. H. Smith pray write to me when you have time adieu my dear Grandpapa believe me to be your affectionate Grand Daughter Eleonora Wayles Randolph.

Dear Grandpapa   Edgehill January 8 1808

I should have written to you post before last but I was not at home and new years day I did write but I did not send the letter because it was not well written as I had bad pens and it was late before I sat down to write. I went sometime ago to a ball given by Mr. Ogilvie and his scholars several of the boys recited pieces some of which were done very well particularly a piece by Peter Pindaur which was spoken by Henry Taylor. An elephant passed through Milton lately Jefferson went to see him but we did not he was only 7 foot high. Aunt Virginia has quitted us Sister Ann spent her Christmas in the North Garden with Cousin Evelina. Papa has returned from Richmond. the orange trees do not look well. Davy let the box that had the geraniums fall out of the cart and break by which means we have lost them. Mama and Sister Ann send their love to you give mine to

Mrs. H. Smith the next time you see her adieu my Dear Grandpapa believe me to be your most affectionate Grand-Daughter Eleonora Wayles Randolph

Dear Grandpapa   Edgehill January 15th 1808
I recieved your letter of the 12 yesterday and am very much obliged to you for the Poetry you sent me. I wrote to you the last post but I did not know when Jefferson went to the post office and he went without it I enclose it to you now. I am sincerely sorry that you have that swelling on your face however I hope it will go down how I long for the time that you are to come home to live and then we shall all go to Monticello to live with you. all is well here. James is well and begins to speak very plain he is the sweetest little fellow you ever saw Mama and Sister Ann send their love to you Cornelia begins to write and I hope will soon be able to write to you. Virginia reads a little in fables of one syllable and Mary can spell. my Bantams are well but I am afraid I shall never raise any adieu my dear Grandpapa believe me to be your affectionate Grand daughter Eleonora Wayles Randolph

Edgehill January 29, 1808
I hardly think it worthwhile to write to you for I have no news nor any thing agreable to tell you but as I know you are always glad to hear from Edgehill I will take up my pen to inform you that all are well here. I am reading Millot in English and Homer's Illiad in English I have begun to study Geography and I am very much pleased with it James grows sweeter and better every day he can speak some words very plain he cannot pronounce my name yet but calls me Ann. Cornelia goes on very well with her writing Virginia and Mary also go on well we have heard lately from Aunt Virginia she says that the embargo has thrown the dissipated inhabitants of Williamsburg in great confusion the Ladies say

they cannot give up tea and coffee and the gentlemen wine. Mama and Sister Ann send their love to you adieu my dear Grandpapa believe me to be your affectionate Grand Daughter

Eleonora Wayles Randolph

> The news conveyed in Ellen's foregoing letter about the "dissipated inhabitants of Williamsburg" and the "ladies who cannot give up tea and coffee and the gentlemen wine," brought a howl of ridicule from Jefferson whose unfortunate Embargo Bill had shut off imports of these pleasing staples. For a time it was considered unpatriotic even to want such luxuries.

My dearest Ellen   Washington Feb. 23.08
I am several letters in your debt, but I am in hopes that age and occupation will privilege me against your counting letter for letter vigorously with me. the loss of your geraniums shall be replaced. I have this day planted a sprig in a small & very portable pot of earth. you give a bad account of the patriotism of the ladies of Williamsburg who are not disposed to submit to the small privations to which the embargo will subject them. I hope this will not be general and that principle & prudence will induce us all to return to the good old plan of manufacturing within our own families most of the articles we need. I can assure you from experience.that we never lived so comfortably as while we were reduced to this system formerly; because we soon learnt to supply all our real wants at home, and we could not run in debt, as not an hour's credit was given for anything. it was then we were obliged to *act* on the salutary maxim of 'never spending our money before we had it'. I expect it will not be long before you will spin me a dimity waistcoat. it is believed Congress will rise early in April: but quite uncer-

tain whether I shall get away then. my swelled face is not yet entirely well. a small knot remains on the bone, which enlarged considerably on my riding out on a raw day lately. by keeping house a few days it is again reduced to a small sore. give my tenderest love to your mama & accept it for yourself and sister.

Th. Jefferson

> Ellen was apparently appalled by Jefferson's facetious suggestion of spinning a dimity waistcoat for him. The twelve-year-old girl had not, she said, spun anything in three years.

Edgehill Feb. 26th 1808

My Dearest Grand Papa must have a bad opinion of my affection for him if he can suppose that I would stand upon ceremony with him and wait for answers to my letters without considering how much he has got to do and how little in comparison I have. it was not anything (I am almost ashamed to confess it) but laziness which I am determined to conquer and pursuant with my Inclination write a long letter every other post (that I am not prevented) to you and will be perfectly satisfied at receiving one every month from you if you will make the agreement I will keep up to it. and often go beyond it by writing sometimes four or five posts hard running and this I will do as often as I can. which will be very frequently as I have but two correspondents besides you and they never write regularly owing perhaps to my not answering their letters till many weeks after I recieve them though they are as bad in that as I am. I fear that I shall never be able to spin you a dimity waistcoat for I cannot now even spin candle wick although I could do it once. it has been 3 years since I have spun any. I have heard lately from Aunt Virginia her little boy and herself are both quite well. Cousin Polly Carr is here at present Cousin Dabneys little daughter had a narrow escape the other day. she was in the yard and she fell down she cried as she had hurt herself a mule was tied near her he broke loose and going to the place where she was stamped on her untill he had broken a silver hook and eye off of her frock when she was carried in the house she was horridly bruised but none of her bones broken.

Cousin Evelina is to be married to Randy Garrett of Charlottesville Mama and Sister Ann send their love to you you must excuse the bad writing of this letter as my pen is shocking adieu my Dear Grandpapa believe me to be your most affectionate Grand Daughter.

E. W. R.

This next letter was, as Jefferson would say in his reply, the best Ellen had ever written him because it was so full of "small news" of family and neighborhood for which he pined.

Edgehill March 11, 1808

In compliance with my promise I take up my pen to write to my Dear Grandpapa. I was disappointed at not recieving a letter from him last post but as I am in hopes I shall get one the next I shall (this being the second week since I have written to you) perform my promise of writing every other post to inform you how we all are. I am in a fair way to raise some Bantams as the hen is now setting she has broken up her residence on the cellar has laid 13 eggs and I hope will hatch some chickens Mr. Ogilvie has broken up keaping school and Jefferson is going to the Green Springs to a Mr. Maury who they say is a very good teacher he knows French and means to teach it. I heard yesterday from Aunt Virginia there has been a horrible riot at Williamsburg 15 boys were expelled and 5 thrown in jail and fined 20. dollars a piece Aunt V.'s child is sick Sister Ann says she would have written but as I write this post you will hear from her the next Mama is a little unwell to day. Sister Ann has had an imposthume on her neck it is well now Aunt Jane's health is still delicate although much better than it has been how is Mrs. H. Smith tell me when you answer this are all the birds and the flowers well I soon will have a garden of my own in which I shall plant the seeds you gave me. the orange trees look very well but one of the finest is dead. we had a visit yesterday from colonel Munroe. Cornelia will soon be in joining hand Virginia reads a little and Mary can spell words of 3 letters she imagines that she is far before Cornelia although she often expresses apprehensions lest Cornelia should catch her and learn to read before she does James is a sweet little fellow speaks quite well and has really grown handsome he thinks of nothing but guns horses and dogs. Mama and sister Ann send their loves to you give mine to Mrs. S. H. S. Cousin Polly Carr has quitted us Mary desires me to tell you that she is spelling c-a-t cat f-a-t fat p-a-t pat and reading "Go-to-Ann-she-is-ill. Jane-has-made-a-nice-plum-tart & will-you-have-some-of-it." Cornelia says will you soon answer her letter she hopes the next you get from her will be in her own hand writing. Virginia sends her love to Francis and yourself. we have not had such a thing as a ball for a long time in Milton and my dancing school is over so that I have not been to a dance for a long time however I never regreted the want of such kinds of amusement although I am fond of dancing. I can always find employments infinitely more amusing and instructing. I am sorry there is so little poetry in the newspapers as my book is not full. if I can fill it Sister Ann and myself will have together an excellent collection. we each have books in which we copy such poetry as we cannot get in newspapers. my Dear Grandpapa will excuse this long catalogue but I have no news to tell him and rather than not write I will relate to him what passes among us which though dull and uninteresting to another will serve to show him that rather than not write at all I will this. all of us are in health Mama since I have been writing has got up off the bed and feels a great deal better. my pen is shocking so that you must excuse the bad writing of this letter adieu my Dear Grand Papa believe me to be your most affectionate Grand Daughter

E.W.R.

My dearest Ellen   Washington Mar. 14.08
Your letter of the 11th is recieved, and is the best letter you have ever written me because it is the longest and fullest of that small news which I have most pleasure in recieving. With great news I am more than surfieted from other quarters, and in order that your letters may not be shortened by a bad pen of which you complain, I have got a pen for you which will be always good, never wearing or needing to be mended. among my books which are gone to Monticello, is a copy of Madame de Sevigne's letters, which being the finest models of easy letter writing, you must read. if Anne & yourself will take it by turns to write by every post, I shall always know of the health of the family, the first object of my concern. I am glad to learn you are at length likely to succeed with your Bantams. They are worthy of your attention. our birds & flowers are well and send their love to yours. Mrs. S. H. Smith is also well, as I learn, for I have not seen her for a long time. She promises to visit us at Monticello this summer. I hope to be with you about the middle or latter part of April. the trumpet of war seems to have frightened the muses from our land & from some other cause they do not get admission into the newspapers of late. I hope this will find your Mama entirely recovered. kiss her warmly

for me, not forgetting the rest of the family. I salute you with love.

Th. Jefferson

Edgehill March 18th 1808

I am glad my Dear Grandpapa expresses approbation at my writing about little things as I always shall have enough to say to you in my letters. I shall be much obliged to you for the pen it will be very convenient and usefull to me as I have a great deal of writing to do pray in your next inform me what it is made of I guess it is glass. I shall certainly read Madame de Sevigne's letters I have heard they were the most elegantly written letters in the world. Cornelia has got in joining hand at last she has begun arithmetic. Virginia goes on tolerably. poor Mary is sick Mama is entirely recovered. I have not yet heard of cousin Evelinas marriage although I suppose it was yesterday as report says that the 17th was the day fixed on. Uncle William is with us now. Mr. Ogilvie has gone to Staunton he is very much ashamed of the indecision he has shown concerning the breaking up of his school he first said he would not then that he would then he was uncertain but at last he has gone away Jefferson has changed his plan he is to remain at home and carry on his arithmetic his geography History Latin and French. James has given the paper a kiss to be sent to you the orange trees still look well I am glad to hear that all your birds and flowers are well we have had one or two violets in bloom and several persian Iris's. we all look forward with great impatience to the time when you are to come back to Monticello how slow time passes away and how heavy it hangs on our hands when we expect to see any one whom we all love as tenderly as we do you. Papa has been to Monticello he says the hall is very beautifull now that it is done. a fire broke out here sometime ago it burnt a mile of fencing and two empty tobacco [barns] this news is very trifling but as you have assured me you like it I shall not hesitate to fill up my letter with it My bantam will hatch in 10 days and I hope I shall raise some of her chickens but they are so delicate she hatched some last year we took great care of them but they died. I am still reading Millot to mama and Justin to myself. Aunt Jane is very well. You are the only correspondent I have and therefore I can write to you very often you desire me to write every other post but I shall sometimes break through that rule and trespass on your patience by writing every post as I have no body else to correspond with and when I get the pen you have given me I shall write a great deal indeed. Harriet Aunt Jane's second daughter has been very ill. and poor little Mary is sick she sends her love to you as do Mama Sister Ann and all the rest of the children they are very much pleased at the thoughts of seeing Francis next summer I think James is a little like him in person. does he curse as much as he used to do formerly all the little ones send their love to him. Give mine to Mrs. S. H. Smith I am very glad to hear she is coming to Monticello I wish to see her again she is a most excellent woman I shall always be gratefull to her for her kindness to me when I was in Washington. I suppose by your saying you have not seen her lately she is in the country. I am very sorry that war has driven the muses away from the United States as I fear my book will never get full. Mama intends to clothe us in homespun this year I shall like it very well. we have had fine weather for a long time which has done a great deal of good to our plants the violets are green and budding one bloomed on the 17th the honeysuckle has several green leaves the orange trees look as fresh and as well as can be. I shall say nothing of Sister Anns charges as she intends herself to give you an account of your tulips tube roses strawberries & & & I do not know how to make an et cetera and therefore you must think there is one after strawberries and not take that awkward mark for one I think my dear Grand Papa you can have no reason to complain of the shortness of this letter as I have spun it out to a great length. I shall therefore bid you adieu and will only subscribe myself my dear Grandpapa your affectionate grand Daughter

E. W. Randolph

Edgehill March 25th 1808

I shall write a few lines to inform my dear Grandpapa that all are well here except James and he is not very sick. all the plants are well we have a great many flowers in bloom Narcissus's Daffodils Hyacinths Periwinkle and a great number of white violets. my bantam will hatch next week. that is all the news I have got to tell you except that Jefferson is going on very well with his studies I am reading Diodorus Siculus [Greek historian] Cornelia goes on tolerably with her writing and Virginia and Mary still continue fond of their books. give my love to Mrs. S. H. S. when you see her next write to me next post my pen is not very good you can perceive by the writing of this letter. Mama Sister Ann and all the children send their love to you adieu my dearest grand Papa and believe me to be your most affectionate GrandDaughter.

Elleonora W. Randolph

My dear Ellen   Washington Mar. 29.08.

I received yesterday yours of the 25th. and have also to acknolege that of the 18th you ask whether the pen which is not to wear out is made of glass? No—guess again. I am glad to hear you expect a family of Bantams. Take good care of them. is it not best to put the hen into a tobacco chick coop in & round which the chickens will always stay. The properest way to make an et.caetera is thus e&c. can you guess why? if you cannot, call Jefferson to your side our newspapers are so barren that I have been obliged to go to Paris for a piece of poetry for you, or at least to a Paris paper. I must here close, being under an attack of periodical head-ach. it began on Friday last Sunday it was severe. yesterday more moderate so that I hope it is on the wane. about an hour in the morning is all the time I have to write in the day. I have given you a part of that. I have kissed this paper, which James must take off with his lips. There is one also for your Mama, yourself and sisters. I bless you all—adieu.

Th. Jefferson

Edgehill April 1 1808

My dear grand papa's letter of the 29th arrived safe yesterday and brought the disagreeable news of his being unwell but we all sincerely wish and hope that he will soon recover and come to see us all again. I will give another guess about the pen it is of steel is it not? my bantam has hatched 8 pretty little chickens and I shall follow your advice about her treatment. the orange trees are well. Sister Ann is gone to Monticello to see about the flowers and plant the berries 3 of your Alpine strawberries are flourishing Mr. Burwell has just sent me some of the seed of the Ice plant I am told it is a very beautifull flower I cannot guess why an et-caetera should be made in the manner you wrote me word if it is not that the figure & represents the E. T. and the C caetera Mama Sister Ann and all the children are quite well and send their love to you adieu my dearest grandpapa believe me to be (with the sincerest wishes for your health) your most affectionate grand daughter

E. W. Randolph

My dearest Ellen   Apr. 12.08.
Your letter of Apr. 1. came to hand only yesterday. I presume you sent it a little too late for the post and that it has lain a

week at Milton. You have guessed rightly both as to the pen and the &. I am entirely recovered of my head-ach. Congress have come to a resolution to adjourn on the 25th of this month. I suppose I shall get away some time in the first week in May. I shall catch you abed I cannot say. we had our first shad here on the 29th of March, and the first asparagus on the 6th of this month. When had you these things? Your letters of the 16th. 23d. & 30th. will still find me here. my affectionate love to everybody.

Th. Jefferson

Edgehill April 14 1808

I have at length guessed right my Dear Grandpapa, about the pen, and am very glad to find it is made of steel. the change in the post, was the cause of your not recieving my letter, of the first of the month, it goes out now much earlier than it formerly did. I am delighted to hear that your head-ach, is over, and that you are to come home so soon. Mr. Mrs. and the two Miss Lindsey's, spent a few days with us; the young ladies, Sister Ann and myself, went over to Monticello; I think the hall, with its gravel colored border is the most beautifull room I ever was in, without excepting the drawing room at Washington. The dining room is also greatly improved; the pillars of the portico are rough cast and look very well; all the railing on the top of the house finished and painted I wont say any thing of the flower bed. that is sister Anns part. The level is spoilt nearly. Mr. Bacon has made a mistake (I presume) and covered it with charcoal, instead of manure; it looks rather dismal where ever the grass has not grown it is quite black, and is excessively dirty to walk on, it is not near as bad as it was but it is still disagreeable and ugly. They are finishing your terrace now. the sheep eat up 48 orange trees and bit half of the finest of besides, when we put them out, however I have 3 tolerably good though they are only 2 inches high they are all mean little things except that which the sheep bit, but they are very young. The third of April snow drops bloomed, you have none I believe. They are very beautifull and I will give you mine if you want them, and have them set in your garden when we go to Monticello. we have had shad the latter end of march; we have got no asparagus beds here and I was so much taken up with looking at the house that I did not inquire about the vegetables at Monticello, besides we stayed but a short time. Aunt Virginia is well. all our family except James are well also. Cornelia was very much delighted with your letter, she easily found out the verse, as she had seen many before of the same kind. Virginia and Mary send their love to you. I am reading Diodorus Siculus. I began to learn Spanish, but I have not said a lesson for a long time, I must take it up again for I wish to know it. I cannot read french entirely without a dictionary yet. adieu my dearest Grandpapa, I am your most affectionate Grand Daughter.

E.W. Randolph.

P.S. I beg you to send the inclosed to Miss Forrest.

My dear Ellen   Washington May 3, .08.
As you insist I shall write you one more letter before my departure. this is to inform you that altho' I have not entirely abandoned the hope of setting out on the 5th, yet I think it more probable I shall be detained to the 6th. so that if I do not catch you in bed on Sunday, expect it on Monday.

Your's affectionately
Th: Jefferson

Always a farmer at heart, climate fascinated Jefferson. For years he kept a daily reading of the thermometer wherever he happened to be. Here, in a letter to Ellen, we find him thanking heaven that the fourth of July was over and giving evidence that the city of Washington was then as hot and sticky in summer as it is today.

My Dear Ellen   Washington, July 5, '08.
Your letter was safely delivered to Miss Forrest who was here yesterday. I thank heaven that the 4th of July is over. It's always a day of great fatigue to me, and of some embarrassments from improper intrusions and some from unintended exclusions. We have had such a week of hot weather as has never probably been known before in this country. My thermometer has been as follows:

Monday	June	27	93
		28	95
		29	96
		30	95
	July	1	98½
		2	98
		3	95½

Yesterday I took no observation, today it is quite moderate. I hope this severe spell will be an acquittal for us, at least till I get home, for which I shall leave this place about the 22 inst. You have been beforehand with us in rostin [roasting] ears, we had cimlings yesterday. Kiss your dear Mama for me and all the young ones, assure your papa of my constant affection, be assured yourself of my tender love,

Th. Jefferson.
P.S. 2 men died here on the 1st instant drinking cold water. We shall probably hear of many more in other places.

Dear Grandpapa   November 11th 1808
I expect every moment that they will come to carry my letters to the post office but still I have begun to write in hopes that I shall conclude my letter before the others are sent away.

The sweet scented grass I shall take all possible care of. the pot was broken on the way It was tied together but I shall have to remove the grass soon in another box. Your Orange trees come on very well, as to their looks, but I never saw such little short things in my life they are near eighteen months old and they are not as high (any of them) as my hand is long. Sister Ann and Mr. Bankhead left us some days before your letter arrived. Benjamins eye is entirely well except the redness which the rising has left. all the family are well and send their love to you I beg you will forward the inclosed to my brother [Jefferson was then studying in Philadelphia]. adieu my dear Grandpapa believe me to be your most affectionate Grand Daughter

E.W.R.

My dear Ellen   Washington Nov. 15.08.
I recieved yesterday yours of the 11th & rejoice to hear that all are well with you. I inclose a letter from Dr. Wistar the perusal of which will be agreeable to your Papa & Mama as it respects Jefferson, & to your Papa what relates to the Mammoth. return it to me. I am glad to hear that the sweetscented grass got safe, altho' the pot did not. The sooner you put it into a larger box the better. perhaps your papa will take the trouble to separate the roots so as to spread without endangering them. it is the anthoxanthum odosatum of the botanist, and you must now become the botanist in addition to your charge over the basse-cour. This last department will be recruited when I come home by 6 wild geese born of tamed parents, 2 summer ducks, a pair of wild turkies, 6 gray geese, much larger & handsomer than the common race of which the ganders are white. for the former department I have 700 species of seeds sent me by Mr. Thouin from the National garden of France. What will you do under all this charge? and more especially as the geese, ducks & will be

very clamorous from daylight till visited. it is lucky for you that the milk pen & sheep-cote from their distance, cannot be ascribed to your care under colour of their belonging to the field of natural history. I sent by Mr. Bacon some corks to compleat the bottling our wines. Was my letter forwarded to Anne? those to Jefferson will go on to-day. affectionate adieux to every body.

Th. Jefferson

My Dear Grandpapa   Edgehill December 15th 1808
With this letter I send you a book which is in a miserable and tattered condition which if you will have bound for me I will be very much obliged to you it is old and rotten but be-ing valuable to me on account of the person who gave it if it can be stuck together any way so as to prevent it from tumbling to pieces it will do. Many of the leaves are lost for it has seen hard service though not since I have had it. Col Lewis died last Thursday night. The sweet scented grass looks very well. it was transplanted carefully in a larger box. My Bantams are very mischievous they have pecked all the leaves off of some fine orange trees they have increased very much. there are at least a peck of Tube rose and 12 or 14 Amaryllis roots all packed in bran. The Geese and ducks shall be attended to when we go to Monticello. The seed I hope will succeed better than those which Sister Ann and yourself planted in the oval beds. The OERAS Wine which was in the little crazy casks is bottled off. there are not bottles enough to draw any other kind but it is no matter for All the rest is perfectly safe. when the book is bound I will thank you to return it for Cornelia to read. all the children send their love to you adieu dear Grandpapa believe me to be your most affectionate Grand daughter

Eleonora W. Randolph

Mama says she will write next post the watch, key and ring came safe. . . .

Skimming through his mail this February morning, 1809, President Jefferson found the letter he was looking for. He had sent some plants down to Monticello several weeks ago. Up to now he had received no word of their safe arrival.

Dear Grandpapa   Edgehill January 26th 1809
I would have written you last post, if I had had time, but I am determined to do it this, although I have not much to say, unless I talk about the plants; those in the large box were killed to the roots, but they are coming up all over the box; those in the small pot were killed also, but are putting out small fresh buds; the evergreens have lost all their leaves but one branch on each, which looks lively enough; in the large pot there is not the least appearance of life, but Mama preserved a little pod full of seed from it. poor James has been inoculated with the Vaccine and is very unwell. Benjamin has had it but he did not have a fever. You must pardon this letter so full of mistakes, for it is written by candle light, I have been writing almost allday, give my love to Mrs. S. H. Smith, the children and mama send theirs to you. I am dear Grand-Papa your most affectionate Grand Daughter
                    Ellenore Wayles Randolph
The sweet scented grass looks very badly although Mama seperated the roots and planted them with great care in a box of fine rich mould and the season in which it was done was warm and rainy
                              Yours affectionately
                              E W R

In about four weeks Jefferson would wind up his eight years in the presidency, but grave problems still con-

fronted him: How to keep the nation out of Britain's war with Napoleon, with their cruisers flouting American neutrality on every ocean? How to hand over his political machine intact to his successor? How to close his long public service with the best of grace? He had money problems, too, for he was retiring burdened with debt. Yet for the moment affairs of state must wait. He would send Ellen a few further facts about the plants. Dipping his quill, he scratched off a hasty letter.

My dear Ellen   Washington Feb. 6.09.
I have received your letter on the subject of my plants and will now explain to you what they were, tho' I cannot say what was in each box or pot particularly.

Savory, a dead plant, it's leaves very aromatic. a little resembling thyme my dependance is that it's seeds are shed on the earth in the box & will come up.

Arbor vitae. a small evergreen tree, in a small pot.

Ice plant. not entirely dead, but I suppose it's seeds shed on the earth & will come up.

Tarragon. a plant of some size. the leaves mostly dead. I expect the seed is shattered & will come up.

Geranium. I think there was a plant of this but am not certain

Besides the above there was a box containing many sods of sweet-scented grass, packed one on another & in the same box a bunch of monthly raspberry plants, which box Davy was directed to carry to Monticello. I must fear he did not, as Bacon writes me he received no raspberry plants, saying nothing of the grass. Kiss every body affectionately for me.

                                                Th: Jefferson

February 20. Jefferson was impatient to hand the reins to his devoted friend and successor, Secretary of State James Madison. March 4 could not come soon enough though

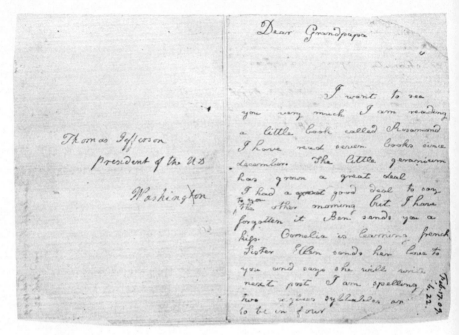

This little note from Virginia Randolph, seven, which Jefferson received on February 17, 1809, was written for her by thirteen-year-old Ellen. (Courtesy of the Massachusetts Historical Society.)

he had innumerable things to do. Boxes of his precious papers and books to be packed and sent off to Monticello; three wagonloads of shrubs and seeds to beautify Monticello. On the President's desk lay a stack of bills passed by

Congress in the last minute rush before adjournment. These must be read and signed or vetoed. Besides, he must keep a watchful eye on Congress, where debate still flared over a substitute for the unfortunate Embargo Bill. But the end was in sight. He would send a last note to Ellen before he took the road to Monticello come mid-March.

My Dear Ellen,   Washington Feb 20 09
My last letter to you stated the plants which had been sent
and I was in hopes after you had been enabled to distinguish
them you would have informed me of their respective condi-
tions but no post has arrived from Milton & consequently no
letter from you in about three weeks I hope to be with you
and then we shall properly be devoted to the garden. what
has become of Mrs. Trist? I have not heard a word from her
since I left Monticello. I enclose you a budget of poetry to be
distributed according to their address. tell your Papa that
the ultimate decision of Congress is as uncertain at this moment as it ever was. I rather believe the embargo will be
repealed the 4th of March & a nonintercourse with France
and England & their dependencies be substituted but it is by
no means certain. my affection to him & kisses to your dear
Mama & sisters. All love to yourself.

Th: Jefferson

For the next sixteen years Jefferson, established at Monticello, enjoyed the companionship of his dear Ellen, as
well as that of the entire Randolph family that had come
to live at Monticello about 1809. Three more children
were born to Martha Randolph in those years. And there
were weddings.

The gardens were aglow with spring flowers when, on
May 25, 1825, Ellen was married at Monticello to the Bos-
tonian Joseph Coolidge, Jr. The year before he had come
to visit Thomas Jefferson and had fallen in love with the
brilliant, and equally charming, Ellen Randolph. Jefferson sanctioned the match, saying to Joseph Coolidge: "I
assure you that no union could give me greater satisfaction." The happy pair rode off for a honeymoon trip that
almost duplicated the "botanizing expedition" Jefferson
and Madison made in 1791—to lakes George and Cham-

plain, across to Vermont, down through Massachusetts and Connecticut and terminating in Philadelphia. But the honeymooners did not wind up their peregrinations at Philadelphia as did the two statesmen. Instead they drew rein finally at Boston, where they would make their home.

The eighty-two-year-old Jefferson of course missed his long-time companion. In August 27, 1825, he writes to her of the University of Virginia, which he was busy founding, reminisces on that trip he and Mr. Madison had taken, and adds movingly:

We did not know until you left us what a void it would make in our family. Imagination had illy sketched its full measure to us; and, at this moment, everything around serves but to remind us of our past happiness, only consoled by the addition it has made to yours. Of this we are abundantly assured by the most excellent and amiable character to which we have committed your future well-being, and by the kindness with which you have been received by the worthy family into which you are now engrafted.

Later that year Jefferson gave a last testimonial of his love for Ellen that now included the man of her choice. The packet on which her baggage and precious keepsakes were shipped to her new home in the North caught fire off the coast and Ellen's treasures, including many of her wedding gifts, went up in flames. Among them was a beautiful, hand-carved writing desk, Jefferson's wedding gift to the bride. It was made by Jefferson's old Negro woodworker, John Hemings, of whose skill he often boasted. John had put into the desk all the artistry he possessed, inlaying it with choicest bits of wood, some rare, others grown on the Monticello hillside.

When Jefferson heard of Ellen's loss, he responded in his typically thoughtful generous way and wrote:

Monticello in the 1850's. Twenty-five years earlier, in 1824, a young New Englander, Joseph Coolidge, came to visit the "Sage of Monticello"—and stayed to lose his heart to the lovely Ellen.

Monticello, November 14, 1825

My Dear Ellen . . . We have heard of the loss of your baggage, with the vessel carrying it, and sincerely condole with you on it. It is not to be estimated by its pecuniary value, but by that it held in your affections,—the documents of your childhood, your letters, your correspondencies, notes, books, etc., etc., all gone! and your life cut in two, as it were, and a new one to begin, without any records of the former. John Hemings was the first who brought me the news. He had caught it accidentally from those who first read the letter from Colonel Peyton announcing it. He was *au desespoir!* That beautiful writing desk he had taken so much pains to make for you! everything else seemed as nothing in his eye, and that loss was everything. Virgil could not have been more afflicted had his Aeneid fallen a prey to the flames. I asked him if he could not replace it by making another. No; his eyesight had failed him too much, and his recollection of it was too imperfect. It has occurred to me, however, that I can replace it, not, indeed, to you, but to Mr. Coolidge, by a substitute, not claiming the same value from its decorations, but from the part it has *borne* in our history and the events with which it has been associated. I received a letter from a friend in Philadelphia lately, asking information of the house, and room of the house there, in which the Declaration of Independence was written, with a view to future celebrations of the Fourth of July in it, another enquiring whether a paper given to the Philosophical Society there, as a rough draught of that Declaration was genuinely so. A society is formed there lately for an annual celebration of the advent of Penn to that place. It was held in his ancient mansion, and the chair in which he actually sat when at his writing table was presented by a lady owning it, and was occupied by the president of the celebration. Two other chairs were given them, made of the elm under the shade of which Penn had made his first treaty with the Indians. If then things acquire a superstitious value because of their connection with particular persons, surely a connection with the great Charter of our Independence may give a value to what has been associated with that; and such was the idea of the enquirers after the room in which it was written. Now I happen still to possess the writing-box on which it was written. It was made from a drawing of my own by Ben. Randall, a cabinetmaker in whose house I took my first lodgings on my arrival in Philadelphia in May, 1776, and I have used it ever since. It claims no merit of particular beauty. It is plain, neat, convenient, and, taking no more room on the writing table

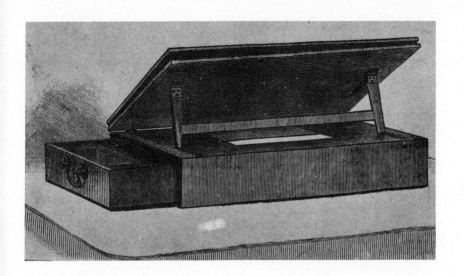

The lap desk on which Jefferson wrote the Declaration of Independence and the accompanying historical note were presented to Ellen and her new husband, Joseph Coolidge, as a "memorial of affection" by Jefferson to console her for the loss of his original wedding gift to the young couple—a beautifully hand-carved writing desk. In 1876—the centennial year of the Declaration of Independence—the Coolidge family presented Jefferson's lap desk to the nation. (Courtesy of the Smithsonian Institution.)

> Th. Jefferson gives this Writing desk to Joseph Coolidge junr. as a memorial of affection. it was made from a drawing of his own. by Ben Randall. cabinet maker of Philadelphia with whom he first lodged on his arrival in that city in May 1776 and is the identical one on which he wrote the Declaration of Independence. Politics as well as Religion has it's superstitions these gaining strength with time, may, one day, give imaginary value to this relic, for it's association with the birth of the Great charter of our Independence.
>
> Monticello. Nov. 18. 1825.

than a moderate quarto volume, it yet displays itself sufficiently for any writing. Mr. Coolidge must do me the favor
of accepting this. Its imaginary value will increase with years,
and if he lives to my age, or another half-century, he may
see it carried in the procession of our nation's birthday, as the
relics of the saints are in those of the Church. I will send it
through Colonel Peyton, and hope with better fortune than
that for which it is to be a substitute. . . .

The year 1826 saw the venerable statesman hastening toward journey's end. Jefferson sensed that his "long serene
day of life" was dimming. In March he composed his will
with its intricate codicil. In early June, Jefferson wrote
his last letter to Ellen:

June 5, 1826
A word to you, my dearest Ellen, under the cover of Mr.
Coolidge's letter. I address you the less frequently, because I
find it easier to write 10 letters of business, than one on the
intangible affections of the mind. were these to be indulged
as calls for writing letters to express them, my love to you
would engross the unremitting exercises of my pen. I hear of
you regularly however, thro' your correspondents of the family, and also of Cornelia since she has joined you. She will
find, on her return some changes in our neighborhood. The
removal of the family of Ashton to New London will be felt
by us all; and will scarcely be compensated by an increased
intercourse with the house beyond them. yesterday closed a
visit of 6 weeks from the younger members of the latter,
during which their attractions had kept us full of the hom-
agers to their beauty. according to appearances they had
many nibbles and bites, but whether the hooks took firm
hold of any particular subject or not, is a secret not commu-
nicated to me. if not, we shall know it by a return to their

angling grounds, for here they fish them until they catch something to their palate. The annual visit of the family en masse begins, you know, the next month. our near relationship of blood interests me of course in their success. for by ascending to my great grandfather to their great, great, great grandfather, we come to a common ancestor.—shall I say anything to you of my health: it is as good as I ever expect it to be. at present tolerable, but subject to occasional relapses of sufferance. I am just now out of one of these. The pleasure of seeing yourself, Mr. Coolidge and Cornelia I begin to enjoy in anticipation; and am sure I shall feel it's sanative effects when the moment arrives.—I commit my affections to mr. Coolidge to my letter to him. communicate those to Cornelia by a thousand kisses from me, and take to yourself those I impress on this paper for you.

Th: Jefferson

On July 4, 1826 he was gone.

I V

Cornelia Jefferson Randolph

1 7 9 9 - 1 8 7 1

"Now you know the value of a goose"

Cornelia Jefferson Randolph was fourth of the eleven Randolph grandchildren who filled Jefferson's later life with love and adoration. Her extant correspondence with her grandfather is meager but delightful.

Apparently Cornelia inherited something of her grandfather's architectural talents. Her skill at sketching appeared early. She could "draw at" anything. She tried her nimble pencil on the dogs, cats, chickens, and horses around Monticello and even on features of the mansion itself. Jefferson encouraged the youthful artist who brought her handiwork to him for criticism and suggestions.

Cornelia's draftsmanship was later to prove most help-

Jefferson "corresponded" with his granddaughter Cornelia Jefferson Randolph before she had mastered the art of letter writing. This is a silhouette of a bust of Cornelia sculptured at Monticello in 1820. (Courtesy of Mrs. Page Kirk, Charlottesville, Virginia; photo by Ed Roseberry.)

ful to him. While he was creating designs for the distinguished buildings that comprised his original "academical village," now the University of Virginia, Cornelia drew many of the architectural elevations of various buildings. From her fine hand came also the elevation and floor plan of Poplar Forest, his unique octagonal hideaway-home some ninety miles southwest of Monticello in which he often took refuge to escape streams of the admiring and curious who "crashed" his privacy at Monticello.

Even before Cornelia learned to write, Jefferson was addressing letters to her. With his first extant letter to her he enclosed for her scrapbook a "piece" he had "learnt" as a boy. She had learned to read a little, but was still trying to master the art of writing.

Washington, April 3, '08.

My Dear Cornelia: I have owed you a letter two months, but have had nothing to write about; till last night I found in a newspaper the four lines which I now inclose you: and as you are learning to write, they will be a good lesson to convince you of the importance of minding your stops in writing. I allow you a day to find out yourself how to read these lines, so as to make them true. If you cannot do it in that time, you may call in assistance. At the same time, I will give your four other lines, which I learnt when I was but a little older than you, and I still remember.

> I've seen the sea all in a blaze of fire
> I've seen a house high as the moon and higher
> I've seen the sun at twelve o'clock at night
> I've seen the man who saw this wondrous sight.

All this is true, whatever you may think of it at first reading. I mentioned in my letter of last week to Ellen, that I was under an attack of periodical headache. This is the 10th day. It has been very moderate, and yesterday did not last more than three hours. Tell your mamma that I fear I shall not get away as soon as I expected. Congress has spent the last five days without employing a single hour in the business necessary to be finished. Kiss her for me, and all the sisterhood. To Jefferson I give my hand, to your papa my affectionate salutations. You have always my love.

Th. Jefferson.

P.S.—April 5. I have kept my letter open till to-day, and am able to say now, that my headache for the last two days has been scarcely sensible.

> Months later Cornelia proudly addressed to her grandfather the first letter she ever wrote. She was nine; he the President of the United States. The double-ruled lines drawn for her guidance by her mother are still visible on the original in the manuscript division of the Alderman Library at the University of Virginia.

Dear Grandpapa   [Received Dec. 19.08.]
I hope you will excuse my bad writing, for it is the first letter I ever wrote, there are a number of faults, in it I know but those you will excuse; I am reading a very pretty little book called dramatic dialogues, that mrs smith gave sister Elen when she was a little girl, I am very much pleased with it. all the children send their love to you we all want to see you very much. adieu my dear Grandpapa, beleive me to be your most affectionate Granddaughter. C. R.

> Jefferson's reply was a masterpiece of letter-writing to a juvenile. The Jefferson to whom he refers was Cornelia's brother Thomas Jefferson Randolph, who had just entered college at Philadelphia.

Washington Dec. 26, 08.

I congratulate you, my dear Cornelia, on having acquired the

Dear Grandpapa
I hope you will excuse my bad writing, for it is the first let=ter I ever wrote, there are a number of faults in it I know, but those you will excuse, I am reading a very pretty little book called dra==matic dialogues, that mrs smith gave sister Ellen when she was a little girl, I am very much pleased with it. all the chil==dren send their love to you we all want to see you very much adieu my dear Grandpapa, beleive me to be your most affectionate Grand=daughter C. R.

Cornelia Jefferson Randolph was nine years old when she actually wrote her first letter to her grandfather. Cornelia's mother, Martha, had double-ruled lines on the paper to guide her hand. (Courtesy of the University of Virginia Library; photo by Ed Roseberry.)

invaluable art of writing. how delightful to be enabled by it to converse with an absent friend, as if present. to this we are indebted for all our reading; because it must be written before we can read it. to this we are indebted for the Iliad, the Aeneid, the Columbiad, Henriad, Dunciad, and now, for the most glorious poem of all, the Tarrapiniad, which I now inclose you. this sublime poem consigns to everlasting fame the greatest atchievement in war ever known to ancient or modern times. in the battle of David & Goliath, the disparity between the combatants was nothing in comparison of our case. I rejoice that you have learnt to write for another reason; for, as that is done with a goose quill, you now know the value of a goose, and of course you will assist Ellen in taking care of the half dozen very fine grey geese which I shall send by Davy. but as to this I must refer to your Mama to decide whether they will be safest at Edgehill or at Monticello till I return home, and to give orders accordingly. I recieved letters a few days ago from mr Bankhead & Anne. they are well. I had expected a visit from Jefferson at Christmas, had there been a sufficient intermission in his lectures. but I suppose there was not, as he is not come. remember me affectionately to your Papa & Mama, & kiss Ellen & all the children for me.

Th. Jefferson.

P.S. since writing the above, I have a letter from mr Peale informing me that Jefferson is well, and saying the best things of him.

> Here are two more of his letters to her: one written shortly before he left the presidency, the other while she was absent from Monticello.

My dear Cornelia   Washington, Jan. 23, '09.
I received by the last post your letter which you desire me to answer by the succeeding one. I have accordingly set down to

Washington Dec. 26. 08.

I congratulate you, my dear Cornelia, on having acquired the invaluable art of writing. how delightful to be enabled by it to converse with an absent friend, as if present. to this we are indebted for all our reading: because it must be written before we can read it. to this we are indebted for the Iliad, the Aeneid, the Columbiad, Henriade, Dunciad, and now for the most glorious poem of all, the tarrapiniad, which I now inclose you. this sublime poem consigns to everlasting fame the greatest atchievement in ever ever known to antient or modern times. in the battle of David & Goliath the disparity between the combatants was nothing in comparison of our case. I rejoice that you have learnt to write for another reason; for, as that is done with a goose quill, you now know the value of a goose, and of course you will assist Ellen in taking care of the half dozen very fine grey geese which I shall send by Davy. but as to this I must refer to your Mama to decide whether they will be safest at Edgehill or at Monticello till I return home, and to give orders accordingly. I received letter a few days ago from mr Bankhead & Anne. they are well. I had expected a visit from Jefferson at Christmas, had there been a sufficient intermission in his lectures. but I suppose there was not, as he is not come. remember me affectionately to your Papa & Mama, & kiss Ellen & all the children for me.

Th Jefferson

P.S. since writing the above I have a letter from mr Peale informing me that Jefferson is well, and saying the best things of him.

"How delightful to be enabled [by writing] to converse with an absent friend," was Jefferson's reply to Cornelia's first letter to him, which Jefferson received on December 19, 1808. (Courtesy of The Library of Congress.)

do it, & to find out the points in your letter to which you wish an answer. they are rather blunt & difficult to ascertain. they seem however to be these. 1. You thank me for the Terrapiniad. to this I answer, you are welcome. 2. You have pasted it in a book. I answer, that is very well. 3. Virginia reads well and sends her love to me. I answer that that is best of all that she is a very good girl, and I return her my love. your letter being now fully answered, I have only to add that I inclose you two pieces for your book, and desire you to kiss your Mama and all the young ones for me with assurances of my tenderest love.

Th. Jefferson.

Monticello, June 3, '11.

My Dear Cornelia: I have lately received a copy of Miss Edgeworth's Moral Tales, which seeming better suited to your years than to mine, I inclose you the first volume. The other two shall follow as soon as your mamma has read them. They are to make a part of your library. I have not looked into them, preferring to receive their character from you, after you shall have read them. Your family of silkworms is reduced to a single individual. That is now spinning his broach. To encourage Virginia and Mary to take care of it, I tell them that as soon as they can get wedding-gowns from this spinner, they shall be married. I propose the same to you; that, in order to hasten its work, you may hasten home; for we all wish much to see you, and to express in person, rather than by letter, the assurance of our affectionate love.

Th. Jefferson.

P.S.—The girls desire me to add a postscript, to inform you that Mrs. Higginbotham has just given them new dolls.

V

Anne Cary Randolph

1 7 9 1 - 1 8 2 6

*"The flowers come forth like the belles
of the day"*

Anne Cary Randolph, oldest of the six Randolph sisters,
was the beauty of the family. Fair-haired, blue-eyed, she
was so lovely that Jefferson once compared her to a gleam
of sunshine. It was of her as a toddler that Jefferson wrote
"even Socrates might ride on a stick with her without being ridiculous."

Born early in 1791, she was the first of Jefferson's grandchildren and her welcome was warm. He was Secretary of
State at Philadelphia at the time. She brought a love of
flowers with her, a love she shared with her grandfather.
She befriended every flower, plant, shrub, and tree with
which Jefferson glorified the grounds around Monticello.
During his long absences from home while President,

Here is Anne Cary Randolph, at twenty-nine, as she looked to William Coffee, who sculptured this bust of her about 1820. (Courtesy of the Thomas Jefferson Memorial Foundation; photo by Ed Roseberry.)

Anne was mistress of the gardens. On his summer vacations she was constantly at his side. With the help of old Wormley, and the overseer, Edmund Bacon, Anne carried out her grandfather's gardening instructions. In winter she watched over the plants and flowers in his "greenhouse," which was the glassed-in piazza adjoining his study. Not too successful was this greenhouse in which the thermometer sometimes dropped to twenty degrees in real cold weather.

In the winter of 1805-1806, Martha Randolph again took her children to Washington to visit the President. Anne, then nearing sixteen, became the toast of the town. She had the added glamour of being the President's granddaughter. Many were the gay, distinguished gallants who paid court to her charm and beauty.

About this time, into her life swaggered handsome, headstrong young Charles Lewis Bankhead, who swept exquisite Anne off her feet. The flashy gentleman, hailing from a North Carolina plantation, breezed into Charlottesville apparently seeking his fortune by making "contacts" with prominent people. He set his sights for Anne the moment he saw her. Anne's parents tried to discourage the match, but Jefferson looked on without interfering: if Anne loved the young man that was her business.

Anne and Charles were married at Monticello shortly before the end of Jefferson's presidency. As a home for the young couple, Jefferson remodeled a barn on his nearby Tufton plantation. Unhappily for Anne, her union was a severe ordeal. Bankhead turned to law only to embark on various drunken escapades, even to riding his horse into a tavern and at another time threatening Burwell with bodily harm unless he gave him the key to the Monticello wine cellar. The marriage lasted long enough to produce Jefferson's first four great-grandchildren.

The scene closed for Anne in February, 1826, at Monticello, a few months before Jefferson himself came to the end of his road. To Anne's brother, Thomas Jefferson Randolph, absent in Richmond, Jefferson sent this touching note:

Monticello, Feb. 11th, '26

Bad news, dear Jefferson, as to your sister Anne. She expired about half an hour ago. I have been so ill for several days that I could not go to see her till this morning, and found her speechless and insensible. She breathed her last about 11 o'clock. Heaven seems to be overwhelming us with every form of misfortune, and I expect your next will give me the *coup de grace*. Your own family are all well. Affectionately adieu.

Th. Jefferson

She was just 35, still lovely.

Not many of Anne's letters to her grandfather or his to her are preserved. She was not an ardent letter-writer, but she was very dear to Jefferson. Here are samplings of the early ones.

This first letter was written in the large, round hand of a child. Anne was eleven when she wrote it.

Dear Grand Papa   Edgehill Feb. 26 1802

I am very glad that I can write to you I hope you are well we are all perfectly recovered from our whooping cough I thank you for the book you sent me I am translating Justin's ancient history I want to see you very much believe me Cornelia sends her love to you and has been trying to write to you adieu my Dear Grand Papa believe me your affectionate Grand Daughter Anne Cary Randolph

Two years later her handwriting had developed a mature style of her own which must have pleased Jefferson who set much store by writing a good hand.

Dear Grand Papa

I am very glad that I can write to you I hope you are well we are all perfectly recovered from our whooping cough I thank you for the book you sent me I am translating Justin's ancient history I want to see you very much believe

me Cornelia sends her love to you
and has been trying to write to you
adieu my Dear Grand Papa believe
me your affectionate Grand
Daughter Anne Cary Randolph

Edgehill Feb. 26 1802

On February 26, 1802, Anne—in her large round hand—wrote this brief
note to her grandfather. Jefferson was always interested in the education
of his young folks, and Anne, even at the age of eleven, was careful to
include a report on the progress of her studies. (Courtesy of the University of Virginia Library.)

My Dear Grand Papa   Edgehill Feb. 14 1804
I received your letter on the 13 of Feb: I am much obliged
to you for it & the poetry also I will very gladly undertake to
write to you every post Jefferson is going to a very good latin
school in the neighbourhood Mama is now in very good
health & her apetite is quite restored she has never been out
yet for fear of catching cold all the children send their love
to you & Francis & we are all delighted to hear that we shall
have the pleasure of seeing you so soon adieu my Dear Grand
Papa your most affectionate Grand daughter A C Randolph
Aunt Virginia sends her love to you also

                                        Edgehill March 22 1805
This is the fourth letter I have written to my Dear Grand
Papa without receiving an answer I suppose you have not received them or else your business prevented your answering
them Mama has been very sick & two of the children but
they are now quite well we heard that you were to set off
from Washington on the 8 of March I wish in your next letter
you will let me know whether it is true adieu my Dear Grand
Papa your most affectionate Grand daughter ACR

                                        Edgehill December 12 1806
I received my Dear Grand Papa's letter and am much
obliged to him for it. The grass fowls and flowers arrived
safe on monday afternoon. I planted the former in a box of
rich earth and covered it for a few nights untill I thought it
had taken root and then by degrees for fear of rendering it
too delicate exposed it again. it looks extremely well indeed.
if you think it will not stand the winter out it is not too late
to take it in. the weather here is very cold our first snow was
between 8 and 10 inches deep before it had melted one fell
of 2 and it is still snowing quite fast. it is the general opinion

that we shall have a hard winter. Mr. Shoemaker has been unwell but is now better. My Peyton has returned well; Mama and the children are well also and send their love to you adieu my Dear GrandPapa believe me to be your sincerely affectionate Granddaughter Ann C Randolph

> Jefferson's next letter includes a passage on a feature of Monticello that has been revived in recent years: a winding walk around the lawn with flower beds on each side.

From yourself I may soon expect a report of your first visit to *Monticello,* [she was then living at her father's home, Edgehill] and of the state of our joint concerns there. I find that the limited number of our flower beds will too much restrain the variety of flowers in which we might wish to indulge, & therefore I have resumed an idea, which I had formerly entertained, but had laid by, of a winding walk surrounding the lawn before the house, with a narrow border of flowers on each side. This would give us abundant room for a great variety. I inclose you a sketch of my idea, where the dotted lines on each side of the black line shew the border on each side of the walk. The hollows of the walk would give room for oval beds of flowering shrubs. (June 7, 1807.)

Edgehill January 22 1808
I have intended to write to My Dear Grand Papa for several posts but we are so much engaged in our lesson's that I had not time. Ellen & myself are learning geography with which I am very much pleased indeed I read Coocks voyages in French & Livy in english besides a lesson in Dufief & my Arethmetic & writing every day. I have not been to Monticello since we came from there but Jefferson was there the other day & says that the green house is not done, both your icehouse & ours are filled. I was at Mrs Lewis's on my way from the North garden

she told me she had saved some of the seed of the Cypress vine for you & some prickly ash trees. the Alpine Strawberries are Doing very well. we were so unfortunate as to lose the Mignonett entirely although Mama devided it between Mrs. Lewis Aunt Jane & herself but none of it seeded Mrs Lewis supposes that the climate is too cold for it for she has had it repeatedly before & it never would seed, we have a plenty of the two kinds of marigold that you gave us. I suppose you have heard that Aunt Lewis is gone to Kentucky with her sons I went to see her before she set off she appeared to be very much pleased with the thoughts of Living with her children. all the children send their love to you Virginia desires me to tell you that she can read & Mary that *she* can read "go up." adieu My Dear Grand Papa it wont be long now thank God before you come home to live with us. believe me to be My Dear Dear Grand Papa your sincerely affectionate Grand Daughter

A C Randolph

My dearest Anne,   Washington, Feb. 16, '08.
I shall not attempt to get any more flower roots and seeds from Philadelphia this season, and must rely entirely on you to preserve those we have by having them planted in proper time. This you will see from McMahon's book, & Mr. Bacon will make Wormley prepare the beds whenever you let him know, so that they may be ready when you go over to set out the roots. The first time I come home I will lay out the projected flower borders around the level so that they shall be ready for the next fall; and in the spring of the next year I will bring home a full collection of root & plants. We shall then have room enough for every thing. . . .

Washington, Dec. 8, 1808.

My Dear Anne,—Your letter of Nov. 26 came safely to hand,

and in it the delicious flower of the Acacia, or rather the Mimosa Nilotica, from Mr. Lomax. The mother tree of full growth which I had when I gave him the small one, perished from neglect the first winter I was from home. Does his produce seed? If it does I will thank him for some, and you to take care of them; although he will think it a vain thing at my time of life to be planting a tree of as slow a growth. In fact the Mimosa Nilotica and Orange are the only things I have ever proposed to have in my green house. I like much your choice of books for your winter's reading. Middleton's Life of Cicero is among the most valuable accounts we have of the period of which he writes; and Tacitus I consider as the first writer in the world without a single exception. His book is a compound of history and morality of which we have no other example. In your arithmetic, if you keep yourself familiar with the four elementary operations of addition, subtraction, multiplication, and division, or rather of addition and division, because this last includes subtraction and multiplication, it is as much as you will need. The rule of three, of universal utility, is a thing of mere common-sense; for if one yard of cloth costs three dollars, common-sense will tell you that twenty yards will cost twenty multiplied by three. I inclose you a letter from Jefferson, which I presume will inform you he is well. Present my respects to Mr. Bankhead, and the good family you are with; also to my ancient and intimate friend Mr. Lomax when you have the opportunity. To yourself my affectionate love.

Th. Jefferson

Anne was married and gone from the Monticello circle when Jefferson retired from the presidency. He missed her sorely. Late that year he wrote her, bemoaning, "What is to become of our flowers?"

Monticello, Dec. 29th, 1809.

My dear Anne—Your mamma has given me a letter to inclose to you, but whether it contains any thing contraband I know not. Of that the responsibility must be on her; I therefore inclose it. I suppose she gives you all the small news of the place—such as the race in writing between Virginia and Francis, that the wild geese are well after a flight of a mile and a half into the river, that the plants in the greenhouse prosper, etc., etc. *A propos* of plants, make a thousand acknowledgments to Mrs. Bankhead for the favor proposed of the Cape jessamine. It will be cherished with all the possible attentions; and in return proffer her calycanthuses, pecans, silk-trees, Canada martagons, or any thing else we have. Mr. Bankhead, I suppose, is seeking a merry Christmas in all the wit and merriments of Coke upon Littleton. God send him a good deliverance! Such is the usual prayer for those standing at the bar. Deliver to Mary my kisses, and tell her I have a present from one of her acquaintances, Miss Thomas, for her—the minutest gourd ever seen, of which I send her a draught in the margin. What is to become of our flowers? I left them so entirely to yourself, that I never knew any thing about them, what they are, where they grow, what is to be done for them. You must really make out a book of instructions for Ellen, who has fewer cares in her head than I have. Every thing shall be furnished on my part at her call. Present my friendly respects to Dr. and Mrs. Bankhead. My affectionate attachment to Mr. Bankhead and yourself, not forgetting Mary.

Th. Jefferson

My dear Anne   Monticello May 26.11.
I have just received a copy of the Modern Griselda which Ellen tells me will not be unacceptable to you. I therefore inclose it. The heroine presents herself certainly as a perfect model of ingenious perverseness. & of the art of making herself and others unhappy. if it can be made of use in inculcat-

My dear Anne   Monticello May 26. 11.

    I have just recieved a copy of the Modern Griselda which Ellen tells me will not be unacceptable to you. I therefore inclose it. the heroine presents herself certainly as a perfect mo- -del of ingenious perverseness, & of the art of making herself and others unhappy. if it can be made of use in inculcating the vir- -tues and felicities of life, it must be by the rule of contraries. nothing new has happened in our neighborhood since you left us. the houses & trees stand where they did. the flowers come forth like the belles of the day, have their short reign of beauty and splendor, & retire like them to the more interesting office of reproducing their like. the hyacinths and tulips are off the stage, the Irises are giving place to the Belladonnas, as these will to the Tuberoses &c. as your Mama has done to you, my dear Anne, as you will do to the sisters of little John. and as I shall soon & chearfully do to you all in wishing you a long, long, goodnight. present me respectfully to Doctr. & mrs Bankhead and accept for mr Bankhead & yourself the assurances of my cordial affection, not forgetting that Cornelia shares them.

      Mrs. Anne C. Bankhead.   Th:Jefferson

"The houses & trees stand where they did," wrote Jefferson to Anne in *1811*. She was now married to Charles Lewis Bankhead and living on Jefferson's nearby Tufton plantation. Anne, who had inherited her grandfather's devotion to flowers, eagerly awaited news of her beloved Monticello. (Reproduced by permission of Harold Jefferson Coolidge, Washington, D.C.)

ing the virtues and felicities of life, it must be by the rule of contraries. nothing new has happened in our neighborhood since you left us. The houses & trees stand where they did. The flowers come forth like the belles of the day, have their short reign of beauty and splendor, & retire like them to the more interesting office of reproducing their like. The hyacinths and tulips are off the stage. The Irises are giving place to the Belladonnas, as this will to the Tuberoses Etc. as your Mama has done to you, my dear Anne, as you will do to the sisters of little John, and as I shall soon & chearfully do to you all in wishing you a long, long, goodnight. present me respectfully to Doctr. & mrs Bankhead and accept for mr Bankhead & yourself the assurances of my cordial affection, not forgetting that Cornelia shares them.

Th. Jefferson

VI

Thomas Jefferson Randolph

1 7 9 2 - 1 8 7 5

*"Be very select in the society you attach
yourself to . . . and you will find your
path more easy and tranquil"*

Of Jefferson's twelve grandchildren his favorite was his
namesake, Thomas Jefferson Randolph, oldest son of his
daughter, Martha Randolph. On this grandson Jefferson
lavished a world of love and affection. To him, near the
close of life, Jefferson said, "Yourself particularly, dear
Jefferson, I consider as the greatest of Godsends which
heaven has granted me."

Born in 1792, young Randolph grew into a colossus of
a man. His strength was prodigious and his stature greater
than that of huge Peter, Jefferson's father, who broke the
wilderness surrounding Monticello and set the Jefferson

stamp on the land. This grandson, as Jefferson's executor, assumed the crushing debt left by the great statesman and paid it off, in time, to the last penny.

Jefferson had a passion for the education of youth. He was in reality a teacher. His interest in his grandchildren's education began in their childhood. In a day when the education of women was limited, a friend wrote asking Jefferson's views on female education. He replied, "A plan of female education has never been a subject of systematic contemplation with me. It has occupied my attention so far as only the education of my own daughters occasionally required. Considering that they would be placed in a country situation where little aid could be obtained from abroad, I thought it essential to give them a solid education, which might enable them—when become mothers—to educate their own daughters, and even to direct the course for sons, should their fathers be lost, or incapable, or inattentive. My surviving daughter accordingly, the mother of many daughters as well as sons, has made their education the object of her life. . . ."

Martha Randolph was her children's first schoolmistress. Once a brilliant student at the Panthemont during her father's ministry in Paris, she spoke French fluently. An hour a day in her schoolroom at Edgehill or Monticello was devoted to French. Besides the three R's, she taught them history and literature. Skilled at the harpsichord, she instilled in her children the love and rudiments of music "not so much as an accomplishment as a resource in solitude."

Jefferson took a deep personal interest in the higher education of his first two grandsons. The advent of their college days inspired some of his most valuable observations on education, character and high moral standards.

One of Jefferson's first letters to his namesake was written during his first term in the presidency when the boy was eleven.

This portrait of Thomas Jefferson Randolph, at sixteen, was painted by Charles Willson Peale in 1808. Peale and Jefferson were friends, and Peale befriended the youth when he went to Philadelphia. (Courtesy of Mr. Arthur Rotch, Milton, Massachusetts.)

Washington, Feb. 21st, 1803.
I have to acknowledge the receipt of your letter of the 3d,
my dear Jefferson, and to congratulate you on your writing
so good a hand. By the last post I sent you a French Grammar,
and within three weeks I shall be able to ask you, "Parlez
vous Francais, monsieur?" I expect to leave this about the 9th,
if unexpected business should not detain me, and then it
will depend on the weather and the roads how long I shall
be going—probably five days. The roads will be so deep that
I can not flatter myself with catching Ellen in bed. Tell her
that Mrs. Harrison Smith desires her compliments to her.
Your mamma has probably heard of the death of Mrs. Bar-
rows. Mrs. Brent is not far from it. Present my affections to
your papa, mamma, and the young ones, and be assured of
them yourself.

Th. Jefferson.

Jefferson's active interest in young Tom Jefferson Randolph's education began in 1808 when, at fifteen, the boy
went off to college in Philadelphia to attend lectures
in anatomy, botany, and astronomy. On his way Tom
stopped off at Washington to spend a few days with his
grandfather. Jefferson had the lad unpack his trunk and
spread out his college wardrobe. After scrutinizing the
outlay closely, Jefferson made a list of the things he
thought a boy going off to college should have. "You will
need these when you get to Philadelphia," he said. Next
day he accompanied Tom to the shops and purchased the
various articles he had listed. Before Tom left he filled his
purse. More than that, Jefferson paid the entire cost of his
stay at college.

In due time the lad notified his grandfather of his arrival at Philadelphia. Jefferson promptly acknowledged
his letter.

Dear Jefferson: Washington, October 24th, 1808.
I inclose you a letter from Ellen, which, I presume, will inform you that all are well at Edgehill. I received yours without date of either time or place, but written, I presume, on your arrival at Philadelphia. As the commencement of your lectures is now approaching, and you will hear two lectures a day, I would recommend to you to set out from the beginning with the rule to commit to writing every evening the substance of the lectures of the day. It will be attended with many advantages. It will oblige you to attend closely to what is delivered to recall it to your memory, to understand, and to digest it in the evening; it will fix it in your memory, and enable you to refresh it at any future time. It will be much better to you than even a better digest by another hand, because it will better recall to your mind the ideas which you originally entertained and meant to abridge. Then, if once a week, you will, in a letter to me, state a synopsis or summary view of the heads of the lectures of the preceding week, it will give me great satisfaction to attend to your progress, and it will further aid you by obliging you still more to generalize and to see analytically the fields of science over which you are travelling. I wish to hear of the commissions I gave you for Rigden, Voight, and Ronaldson, of the delivery of the letters I gave you to my friends there, and how you like your situation. This will give you matter for a long letter, which will give you as useful an exercise in writing as a pleasing one to me in reading.

God bless you and prosper your pursuits.

Th. Jefferson.

Jefferson then waited exactly a month before writing again. Now that the young man was established at college and had begun his studies, Jefferson wrote him a remarkable letter, full of splendid advice, finer perhaps than any he ever wrote to any young man. In this letter, by way of pointing a moral, Jefferson recalled how he himself had avoided becoming a wastrel, harking back to the wild oats of his college days in the gay colonial capital, Williamsburg, and retracing a chapter of his own personal history. Dr. Small and Mr. Wythe were both professors at William and Mary when Jefferson was a student there; Peyton Randolph was president of the First Continental Congress.

My Dear Jefferson,—   Washington, November 24, 1808. Your situation, thrown at such a distance from us, and alone, cannot but give us all great anxieties for you. As much has been secured for you, by your particular position and the acquaintance to which you have been recommended, as could be done towards shielding you from the dangers which surround you. But thrown on a wide world, among entire strangers, without a friend or guardian to advise, so young too, and with so little experience of mankind, your dangers are great, and still your safety must rest on yourself. A determination never to do what is wrong, prudence and good humor, will go far towards securing to you the estimation of the world. When I recollect that at fourteen years of age, the whole care and direction of myself was thrown on myself entirely, without a relation or friend qualified to advise or guide me, and recollect the various sorts of bad company with which I associated from time to time, I am astonished I did not turn off with some of them, and become as worthless to society as they were. I had the good fortune to become acquainted very early with some characters of very high standing, and to feel the incessant wish that I could ever become what they were. Under temptations and difficulties, I would ask myself what would Dr. Small, Mr. Wythe, Peyton Randolph do in this situation? What course in it will insure

The President's Mansion in Washington. Many of Jefferson's young folks visited him here during his term as third President of the United States.

me their approbation? I am certain that this mode of deciding on my conduct, tended more to correctness than any reasoning powers I possessed. Knowing the even and dignified line they pursued, I could never doubt for a moment which of two courses would be in character for them. Whereas, seeking the same object through a process of moral reasoning, and with the jaundiced eye of youth, I should often have erred. From the circumstances of my position, I was often thrown into the society of horse racers, card players, fox hunters, scientific and professional men, and of dignified men; and many a time have I asked myself, in the enthusiastic moment of the death of a fox, the victory of a favorite horse, the issue of a question eloquently argued at the bar, or in the great council of the nation, well, which of these kinds of reputation should I prefer? That of a horse jockey? a fox hunter? an orator? or the honest advocate of my country's rights? Be assured, my dear Jefferson, that these little returns into ourselves, this self-catechising habit, is not trifling nor useless, but leads to the prudent selection and steady pursuit of what is right.

I have mentioned good humor as one of the preservatives of our peace and tranquillity. It is among the most effectual, and its effect is so well imitated and aided, artificially, by politeness, that this also becomes an acquisition of first rate value. In truth, politeness is artificial good humor, it covers the natural want of it, and ends by rendering habitual a substitute nearly equivalent to the real virtue. It is the practice of sacrificing to those whom we meet in society, all the little conveniences and preferences which will gratify them, and deprive us of nothing worth a moment's consideration; it is the giving a pleasing and flattering turn to our expressions, which will conciliate others, and make them pleased with us as well as themselves. How cheap a price for the good will of another! When this is in return for a rude thing said by another, it brings him to his senses, it mortifies and corrects him in the most salutary way, and places him at the feet of your good nature, in the eyes of the company. But in stating prudential rules for our government in society, I must not omit the important one of never entering into dispute or argument with another. I never saw an instance of one of two disputants convincing the other by argument. I have seen many, on their getting warm, becoming rude, and shooting one another. Conviction is the effect of our dispassionate reasoning, either in solitude, or weighing within ourselves, dispassionately, what we hear from others, standing uncommitted in argument ourselves. It was one of the rules which, above all others, made Doctor Franklin the most amiable of men in society, "never to contradict anybody." If he was urged to announce an opinion, he did it rather by asking questions, as if for information, or by suggesting doubts. When I hear another express an opinion which is not mine, I say to my-self, he has a right to his opinion, as I to mine; why should I question it? His error does me no injury, and shall I become a Don Quixote, to bring all men by force of argument to one opinion? If a fact be misstated, it is probable he is gratified by a belief of it, and I have no right to deprive him of the gratification. If he wants information, he will ask it, and then I will give it in measured terms; but if he still believes his own story, and shows a desire to dispute the fact with me, I hear him and say nothing. It is his affair, not mine, if he pre-fers error. There are two classes of disputants most frequently to be met with among us. The first is of young students, just entered the threshold of science, with a first view of its out-lines, not yet filled up with the details and modifications which a further progress would bring to their knowledge. The other consists of the ill-tempered and rude men in so-ciety, who have taken up a passion for politics. (Good humor and politeness never introduce into mixed society, a ques-tion on which they foresee there will be a difference of opin-ion.) From both of these classes of disputants, my dear Jeffer-son, keep aloof, as you would from the infected subjects of yellow fever or pestilence. Consider yourself, when with them, as among the patients of Bedlam, needing medical more than moral counsel. Be a listener only, keep within yourself, and endeavor to establish with yourself the habit of silence, especially on politics. In the fevered state of our coun-try, no good can ever result from any attempt to set one of these fiery zealots to rights, either in fact or principle. They are determined as to the facts they will believe, and the opin-ions on which they will act. Get by them, therefore, as you would by an angry bull; it is not for a man of sense to dispute the road with such an animal. You will be more exposed than others to have these animals shaking their horns at you, because of the relation in which you stand with me. Full of political venom, and willing to see me and to hate me as a chief in the antagonist party, your presence will be to them what the vomit grass is to the sick dog, a nostrum for producing ejaculation. Look upon them exactly with that eye, and pity them as objects to whom you can administer only occasional ease. My character is not within their power. It is in the hands of my fellow citizens at large, and will be consigned to honor or infamy by the verdict of the republican mass of our country, according to what themselves will have seen, not what their enemies and mine shall have said. Never, therefore, consider these puppies in politics as requiring any notice from you, and always show that you are not afraid to leave my character to the umpirage of public opinion. Look steadily to the pursuits which have carried you to Philadelphia, be very select in the society you attach yourself to, avoid taverns, drinkers, smokers, idlers, and dissipated persons generally; for it is with such that broils and contentions arise; and you will find your path more easy and tranquil. The limits of my paper warn me that it is time for me to close with my affectionate adieu.

Th. Jefferson.

P.S. Present me affectionately to Mr. Ogilvie, and, in doing the same to Mr. Peale, tell him I am writing with his polygraph, and shall send him mine the first moment I have leisure enough to pack it.

Here are two letters from Tom Randolph to his grandfather, written during his first semester at Philadelphia. Also, a letter from Jefferson to him when the boy had finished his lecture courses.

Dear grandfather   Nov 11 [1808]
The introductory lectures have began this week, before I
could attend any lecture at the University I was obliged to
Matriculate, that is, to become a student of Medicine, which
cost 4$ & Dr. Phisick raised his ticket to 15$, Dr. Wistar
would not recieve any thing for his & he says I must attend
Dr. Woodhouse untill he hears from you. I have purchased
Bells Anatomy at 22$ being the only one for sale in the
united states. Your bridle is plated tolerable well & will go
in the packet with the lamp, Dr. Say has your watch. I wish to
join the desecting [dissecting] class if you have no objections,
the expense will be 15 or 20$

                                        yours sincerely [TJR]

Dear Grandfather   Dec. 28 [1808]
I heard to day from a Virginia student who had recieved letters from home stating an Insurrection in Amherst. If you
have heard any of the circumstances attending it, pray inform me, as it is too near to every thing which is dear to me,
to fail being very interesting. I have paid Mr. Wister & Mr.
Parke for [. . .] history, which you had forgot to mention, I
went to see Mr. T. Pemberton, he mentioned he had made
you present of the book & I thought after what he said that
I had better not offer him the Money. You were informed no
doubt by Mr. Peales letter that your remittances were larger
than necessary

                                        Yours affectionately
                                                    TJR
NB. When I had more time, I wrote more intelligibly & more
lengthy.

Dear Jefferson   Monticello June 20.09
In the even current of a country life few occurrences arise of

sufficient note to become the subject of a letter to a person at a distance. it would be little interesting to such an one to be told of the distressing draught of the months of April & May, that wheat & corn scarcely vegetated and no seed in the garden came up; that since that we have had good rains but very cold weather, so that prospects are disheartening for the farmer & little better to the gardener etc. etc. yet these circumstances excite a lively interest on the spot, & in their variations from bad to good & the reverse fills up our lives with those sensations which attach us to existence, altho' they could not be the subject of a letter to a distant friend. hence we write to you seldom, & now after telling you we are all well, I have given you all our news which would be interesting to you. but tho' we do not write, we think of you, & have been for some time counting the days before you will be with us. the death of Dr. Woodhouse & loss of his lectures leave no inducement to protract your stay after the Botanical lectures are ended, for I do not think the mineralogical course important enough for that. we shall expect you therefore when the botanical course is finished, in the mean time it is necessary I should know the state of your funds. before. I left Washington I remitted to Mr. Peale what I supposed would suffice during your stay. but having made some draughts on you, & the one for Lemaire more considerable than I had expected, there will probably be a deficiency. Your Mama desires you will get for Mary a little book she has seen advertised, called the Adventures of Mary & her cat. anticipating the pleasure of your return, & assuring you of the happiness it will give us to have you again among us, to the salutations of the family I add only my own affectionate adieu.

Th. Jefferson

After college Tom became a successful and vigorous

Dear grandfather

The introductory lectures have began this week, before I could attend any lecture at the University I was obliged to Matriculate, that is, to become a student of Medicine, which cost 48$ Dr Phisick raised his ticket to 15$ Dr Wistar would not recieve any thing for his ticket & he says I must attend Dr Woodhouse untill he hears from you. I have purchased Bells Anatomy at 22$ being the only one for sale in the united states. your bridle is plated tolerable well & will go in the packet with the lamps, Dr Say has your watch I wish to join the disecting class if you have no objections, the expense will be 15 or 20$

yours sincerely

After his arrival in Philadelphia, in 1808, young Thomas Randolph re-ported to his grandfather on his first week of introductory lectures. Mindful of his grandfather's instructions on frugality, Tom listed his current expenses—but forgot to sign the letter. (Courtesy of the University of Virginia Library; photo by Ed Roseberry.)

farmer. To him Jefferson later committed the management of his muddled personal and farm affairs.

Jefferson's last letter to his grandson exhibits the "saddest page in his personal history," as touching as any that ever flowed from his pen. The end of life was just around the corner. For years he had lived beyond his means. Now in dire financial straits, his spirits crushed, his dream of a serene old age among those he loved broken, he saw himself and family beggared and evicted from Monticello. In his extremity he appealed to the Virginia legislature to permit him to sell his lands by lottery. He was rich in acreage, but land values were deeply depressed by the financial crisis that had swept the country. He was at the last breach. A lottery would, he thought, save the day. It would enable him to stave off bankruptcy, pay his pressing debts and retain Monticello and a farm or two. But the legislature replied with a flat no.

This last letter acknowledged one from his grandson, who had gone to Richmond to press the matter before the legislature, informing him that his lottery request would be denied. Here Jefferson portrays his agonized feelings. On the day he wrote his letter, his oldest granddaughter, the "dear little Anne" of his letters long ago, was dying at Monticello with only three days of life left to her.

My Dear Jefferson: Monticello, February 8, '26.
I duly received your affectionate letter of the 3d, and perceive there are greater doubts than I had apprehended, whether the Legislature will indulge my request to them. It is a part of my mortification to perceive that I had so far overvalued myself as to have counted on it with too much confidence. I see in the failure of this hope, a deadly blast of all my peace of mind, during my remaining days. You kindly encourage me to keep up my spirits; but oppressed with disease, debility, age, and embarrassed affairs, this is difficult.

For myself I should not regard a prostration of fortune, but I am overwhelmed at the prospect of the situation in which I may leave my family. My dear and beloved daughter, the cherished companion of my early life, and nurse of my age, and her children, rendered as dear to me as if my own from having lived with me from their cradle, left in a comfortless situation, hold up to me nothing but future gloom; and I should not care were life to end with the line I am writing, were it not that in the unhappy state of mind which your father's misfortunes have brought upon him, I may yet be of some avail to the family. Their affectionate devotion to me makes a willingness to endure life a duty, as long as it can be of any use to them. Yourself, particularly, dear Jefferson, I consider as the greatest of the godsends which heaven has granted to me. Without you, what could I do under the difficulties now environing me? These have been produced, in some degree, by my own unskillful management, and devoting my time to the service of my country, but much also by the unfortunate fluctuation in the value of our money, and the long continued depression of farming business. But for these last I am confident my debts might be paid, leaving me Monticello and the Bedford estate; but where there are no bidders, property, however great, is no resource for the payment of debts; all may go for little or nothing. Perhaps, however, even in this case, I may have no right to complain, as these misfortunes have been held back for my last days, when few remain to me. I duly acknowledge that I have gone through a long life, with fewer circumstances of affliction than are the lot of most men—uninterrupted health—a competence for every reasonable want—usefulness to my fellow-citizens—a good portion of their esteem—no complaint against the world which has sufficiently honored me, and above all, a family which has blessed me by their affections, and never by their conduct given me a moment's pain —and should this, my last request, be granted, I may yet close with a cloudless sun a long and serene day of life. Be assured, my dear Jefferson, that I have a just sense of the part you have contributed to this, and that I bear you unmeasured affection.

Th. Jefferson

VII

Francis Wayles Eppes

1 8 0 1 - 1 8 8 1

*"If you dont answer this leter I shant
write you any more"*

The above delicious, boyish threat was addressed to his
fond and distinguished grandsire by Francis Eppes, age
twelve, only surviving child of Jefferson's deceased daughter, Maria.

But read the whole letter *just* as the lad wrote it and
another that had preceded it:

Dear Grandpapa   Lynchburg April 1813
I wish to see you very much I am very sorry that you wont
write to me this leter will make twice I have wrote to you
and if you dont answer this leter I shant write to you any
more I have got through my latin Gramer and I am going

through again I enclose a leter in this from my Cousin Wale Baker Give my love to all the family

> Believe me to remain with filial love
> your most affectionate
>
> Grand Son Francis Eppes

Dear Grand Papa I wish to see you very much I am sorry you did not answer my letter give my love to aunt Randolph [Martha] and all the children, believe me to be your most affectionate

> Grandson Francis Eppes

After the death of the boy's mother, Jefferson had contrived to keep orphan Francis as close to him as he could, either at Monticello, or a school close by, or in the presidential mansion at Washington and sometimes at Poplar Forest, Jefferson's hideway home that he built after he left the President's mansion.

Jefferson dutifully reported the boy's welfare to his father, Jack Eppes, now in Congress and remarried. In 1809, when Francis, at eight, visited Monticello, Jefferson duly notified Francis' father in this humorous wise:

I should sooner have informed you of Francis' safe arrival here. . . . Francis has enjoyed constant and perfect health, and is as happy as the day is long. He has had little success as yet with either his traps, or bow and arrows. He is now engaged in a literary contest with his cousin, Virginia [Randolph], both having begun to write together. As soon as he gets to z (being now only at *h*), he promises you a letter.

When Francis, at fifteen, went off to a pre-college academy, Jefferson shouldered most of the expense of the venture, though he could ill afford to do so. Even at this distance the results of his unsuccessful management of his

Jefferson had a special affection for his grandson Francis Wayles Eppes—the only surviving child of Maria. Here twelve-year-old Francis threatens to stop writing unless Jefferson answers his letters—and he signs his name with a grand flourish. (Courtesy of the University of Virginia Library; photo by Ed Roseberry.)

farms was beginning to close in on him. Shortly after Francis reached the academy Jefferson wrote him a letter in which he condensed his ideas on education, pointing out that an educated gentleman must have something besides book learning. The oft-missing essential was character.

Monticello, May 21, 1816

I send you, my dear Francis, a Greek grammar, the best I know for the use of schools. It is the one now the most generally used in the United States. I expect you will begin it soon after your arrival at the New London Academy [in North Carolina]. You might, while at home, amuse yourself with learning the letters, and spelling and reading the Greek words, so that you may not be stopped by that when Mr. Mitchell puts you into the grammar. I think you will like him, and old Mr. and Mrs. Deshavens, from the character I have of them. I am sure Mr. Mitchell will do everything for you he can, and I have no fear that you will not do full justice to his instruction. But, while you endeavor, by a good store of learning, to prepare yourself to become a useful and distinguished member of your country, you must remember that this can never be, without uniting merit with your learning. Honesty, disinterestedness, and good nature are indispensable to procure the esteem and confidence of those with whom we live, and on whose esteem our happiness depends. Never suffer a thought to be harbored in your mind which you would not avow openly. When tempted to do anything in secret, ask yourself if you would do it in public; if you would not, be sure it is wrong. In little disputes with your companions, give way rather than insist on trifles, for their love and the approbation of others will be worth more to you than the trifle in dispute. Above all things, and at all times, practise yourself in good humor; this of all human qualities is the most amiable and endearing to society. When-ever you feel a warmth of temper rising, check it at once, and suppress it, recollecting it would make you unhappy within yourself, and disliked by others. Nothing gives one person so great an advantage over another, under all circum-stances. Think of these things, practise them, and you will be rewarded by the love and confidence of the world. I have some expectation of being at Poplar Forest the third week of June, when I hope I shall see you going on cleverly, and al-ready beloved by your tutors, curators, and companions, as you are by yours affectionately,

Th. Jefferson.

The "Leschot" to whom Jefferson referred in opening this next letter to Francis was the Swiss clockmaker, Louis Leschot, whom Jefferson brought to Monticello. Leschot made the famous double-faced cannon ball clock that hangs on the wall over the east doorway.

Dear Francis,   Monticello, Jan. 1, 1819.
Leschot has repaired Mrs. Eppes's watch, and changed the pipe of the key, but the watch was so short a time in his hands that she could not be well regulated; she will there-fore probably need further regulation to make her keep good time. I am sorry you are disappointed in your teacher, but it depends on yourself whether this is of any consequence. A master is necessary only to those who require compulsion to get their lessons. As to instruction, a translation supplies the place of a teacher. Get the lessons first by dictionary, and then instead of saying it to a master, go over it with the trans-lation, and that will tell you whether you have got it truly. Dacier's Horace is admirable for this. As to parsing, you can do that by yourself, both as to parts of speech and syntax. You can perfect yourself too in your Greek grammar, as well

alone as with a teacher. Your Spanish, too, should be kept up. All depends on your own resolution to stick as closely to your book as if a master was looking over you. If Dr. Cooper comes to us he will open our Grammar School the 1st of April. We shall be decided in a few days, and I will let you know. . . . Present my respects to Mrs. Eppes, and be assured of my constant affection.

Th. Jefferson.

In this next letter Jefferson refers to his *petit format* library at Poplar Forest, containing several hundred volumes of the smallest sizes obtainable. These books were of British, French, and Italian origin. Included in his *petit format* collection were his favorite Greek and Latin poets in the original. It might be added here that Jefferson willed Poplar Forest to Francis Eppes. It was the only one of his various plantations he was able to pass on to a member of his family.

Dear Francis,   Poplar Forest, Sept. 21, 1820.
I leave at Flood's, with this letter, a packet containing three small volumes, from my *petit format* library, containing several tragedies of Euripides, some of Sophocles, and one of Æschylus. The first you will find easy, the second tolerably so; the last, incomprehensible in his flights among the clouds. His text has come to us so mutilated and defective, and has been so much plastered with amendments by his commentators, that it can scarcely be called his. I inclose you our measured distances expressed in miles and cents. We leave this tomorrow morning, and shall be at Monticello the next night. From there you shall hear from me about the end of the first week of October. By that time I shall either see Dr. Cooper, or know that I shall not see him. I was deceived in the weather the day we left Millbrook. We passed through two hours of very heavy rain, and got to Flood's at 11 o'clock,

where we staid the day. We didn't suffer ourselves, but the servants got very wet. Present our cordial love to the family. Ever and affectionately yours,

Th. Jefferson.

Francis' entrance into South Carolina College in 1820 inspired a series of letters containing many of Jefferson's choicest observations and comments on education.

Dear Francis, Monticello, Oct. 6, 1820.
Your letter of the 28th came to hand yesterday, and as I suppose you are now about leaving Richmond for Columbia, this letter will be addressed to the latter place. I consider you as having made such proficiency in Latin and Greek that, on your arrival at Columbia, you may at once commence the study of the sciences, and as you may well attend two professors at once, I advise you to enter immediately with those of Mathematics and Chemistry; after these go on to Astronomy, Natural Philosophy, Natural History, and Botany. I say nothing of Mineralogy or Geology, because, I presume, they will be comprehended in the Chemical course. Nor shall I say anything of other branches of science, but that you should lose no time on them until the accomplishment of those above-named, before which time we shall have opportunities of further advising together. I hope you will be permitted to enter at once into *a course of mathematics,* which will itself take up all that is useful in Euclid, and that you will not be required to go formally through the usual books of Geometry. That would be a waste of time which you have not to spare, and if you cannot enter the Mathematical school without it, do not enter it at all, but engage in the other sciences above mentioned. Your Latin and Greek should be kept up assiduously, by reading at spare hours; and discontinuing the desultory reading of the schools, I would

advise you to undertake a regular course of History and Poetry, in both languages. In Greek go first through the Cyropaedia, and then read Herodotus, Thucydides, Xenophon's Hellenics and Anabasis. . . . Alexander, and Plutarch's Lives, for prose reading—Homer's Iliad and Odyssey, Euripides, Sophocles, in poetry, and Demosthenes in oratory, alternating prose and verse as most agreeable to yourself. In Latin, read Livy, Caesar, Sallust, Tacitus, Cicero's Philosophies, and some of his orations in prose—and Virgil, Ovid's Metamorphoses, Horace, Terence and Juvenal for poetry; after all these, you will find still many of secondary grade to employ future years, and especially those of old age and retirement. Let me hear from you as soon as you shall have taken your stand in college, and give me a general view of the courses pursued there, and from time to time afterwards advise me of your progress. I will certainly write to you occasionally; but you will not expect it very frequently, as you know how slowly and painfully my stiffened wrist now permits me to write, and how much I am oppressed by a general and revolting correspondence, wearing me down with incessant labor, instead of leaving me to the tranquil happiness with which reading and lighter occupations would fill pleasantly what remains to me of life. I had written to Dr. Cooper that I should leave Monticello for Poplar Forest, about the 11th of this month. He informs me he cannot be here so soon as that, but will call on me at Poplar Forest in the third week of the month. Adieu, my dear Francis. Consider how little time is left you, and how much you have to attain in it, and that every moment you lose of it is lost for ever. Be assured that no one living is more anxious than myself to see you become a virtuous and useful citizen, worthy of the trusts of your country, and wise enough to conduct them advantageously, nor any one more affectionately yours.

Th. Jefferson.

Dear Francis: Poplar Forest, Dec. 13, 1820.
Yours of Oct. 31st, came to me here Nov. 28th, having first
gone to Monticello. I observe the course of reading at Columbia which you note. It either is, or ought to be, the rule of
every collegiate institution to teach to every particular student the branches of science which those who direct him
think will be useful in the pursuits proposed for him, and to
waste his time on nothing which they think will not be useful to him. This will certainly be the fundamental law of
our University, to leave every one free to attend whatever
branches of instruction he wants, and to decline what he
doesn't want. If this be not generally allowed at Columbia, I
hope they may be induced to indulgence in your case, in consideration of the little time you have left, and which you cannot afford to waste on what will be useless to you, or can be
acquired by reading hereafter without the aid of a teacher.
As I do not know any professors at Columbia but Dr.
Cooper, request in my name his interest and influence to be
permitted to adapt your studies to your wants. Reviewing
what you say are the courses of the four classes, I pass over the
1st and 2d, which you are done with, and should select
for you from the 3d, Algebra, Geometry, Trigonometry,
and Natural Philosophy; and from the 4th, Logarithms and
Chemistry, to which I should add Astronomy, Botany, and
Natural History, which you do not mention in any of the
classes. I omit Blair's Rhetoric, Watt's Logic, Kaimes, Paley,
Butler, etc., which you can read in your closet after leaving
college, as well as at it. And in Mathematics I do not think
you have time to undertake either Conic Sections or Flux-
ions. Unless you can be indulged in this selection I shall lament very much indeed, the having advised your going to
Columbia, because time is now the most pressing and precious thing in the world to you, and the greatest injury which

can possibly be done you is to waste what remains on what you can acquire hereafter yourself, and prevent your learning those useful branches which cannot well be acquired without the aids of the college. Whether our University will open this time twelve-month or be shut up seven years, will depend on the present Legislature's liberating our funds by appropriating $100,000 more from the Literary Fund. If you watch the newspapers you will see what they do, and be able to judge what may be expected. Ellen and Virginia are here with me. We leave this the day after to-morrow for Monticello, where we hope to meet your aunt, who will be returning at the same time from Richmond. We learn by your letter to Virginia, that Wayles is with you. To him and to yourself I tender my affectionate attachment. To Dr. Cooper also, give my friendly souveirs; the difficulty with which I write puts that much out of my power.

Th. Jefferson

To Francis the next letter gave a brief preview of the "establishment" he was at the moment "fashioning and fostering for the instruction of those who are to come after us." He referred, of course, to the University of Virginia.

Dear Francis: Monticello, June 27th, 1821.
Your letter of May 7th was received in due time, and in it you ask my opinion as to the utility of pursuing metaphysical studies. No well educated person should be entirely ignorant of the operations of the human mind, to which the name of metaphysics has been given. There are three books on this subject, Locke's Essay on the Human Understanding, Tracy's Elements of Ideology, and Stewart's Philosophy of the Human Mind; any one of which will communicate as much on the subject as is worth attention. I consider Tracy as the most

correct metaphysician living; and I inclose you a small tract of his worth reading, because it is short, profound, and treats an interesting question, to wit, that on the certainty of human knowledge. He prostrates the visions of Malebranche, Berkeley, and other skeptics, by resting the question on the single basis of "We Feel." With him who denies this basis there can be no ground of reasoning at all. To pursue the science further is following a will-of-the-wisp, and a very useless waste of time, much better given to sciences more palpable, and more useful in the business of life. Tracy's Review, or Commentaries on Montesquieu is the best elementary book on government which has ever been published. Being afraid to publish it in France, he sent his manuscript to me, 1809, and I got it translated and published in Philadelphia in 1811. It will be the text-book of the political lectures of the University. The buildings of the University (except the library) will all be finished the ensuing winter. Towards this object the Legislature permitted an advance of $120,000 from the Literary Fund, but under the name of a loan, taking in pledge our annuity of $15,000. If it is to be really redeemed by this, many years will be necessary to clear that fund, but it is hoped they will consider it as an appropriation, and discharge the annuity. Within one year after that discharge, we may open the institution, as it will require that time to bring our professors into place. Mr. Watts when here asked me for a copy of the report containing the plan of that institution; I did not know then that I had a spare copy; I have since found one which I inclose for his acceptance, with the tender of my great respect. Our family is all well, remember you always with affection, and join me in hope you will be able to visit us during your next vacation, as they do in assuring you of our constant attachment.

Th. Jefferson

Dear Francis: Monticello, April 9, 1822.
Your letter of March 22d did not reach me till a few days
ago; that of Feb. 6th had been received in that month. Being
chiefly a statement of facts it did not seem to require an
answer, and my burden of letter-writing is so excessive as to
restrain me to answers absolutely necessary. I think with
you that you had now better turn in to the study of the law.
As no one can read a whole day closely on any one subject to
advantage, you will have time enough in the other portions
of the day to go on with those essential studies which you
have not as yet completed. If you read law from breakfast
four or five hours, enough will remain before dinner for exercise. The morning may be given to Natural Philosophy and
Astronomy, the afternoon to Rhetoric and Belles Lettres,
and the night to history and ethics. The first object will be
to procure the necessary law-books for reading. They will
come twenty-five per cent. cheaper from England than
bought here, and some indeed can only be had there. I will
subjoin a catalogue of what should be obtained as soon as
practicable, and their cost there. About as much the next
year will be a sufficient library for reference in practice. The
course of reading I should advise, would be Coke's Littleton,
and his other Institutes. Bacon's Abridgment, Blackstone's
Commentaries, Woodson's Lectures, and Reeves in Common
Law; and in Chancery, the abridgment of cases in equity,
Bridgman's Digested Index, and Fonblanque, interspersing
some select case from the reporters both in law and equity.
The course will employ two years to be superficial, and three
to be profound. This may be done at Millbrook or Monticello as well as in the lawyer's office. You know, of course,
that you are as much at home at Monticello as at Millbrook,
so that you can choose freely, or divide your time between
them to your own wish. You would have perhaps less inter-
ruption by company at Millbrook, but access here to books

which may not be there. I have fortunately just received from England, Thomas's Coke's Littleton, a most valuable work. He has arranged Coke's matter in the method of Blackstone, adding the notes of Lords Hale and Nottingham and Hairgraves, adding also his own which are excellent. It is now, beyond question, the first elementary book to be read—as agreeable as Blackstone, and more profound. This will employ you fully till the other books can be received from England. They will cost there about $200, to which is to be added duties, about thirty dollars freight and charges. If I can be useful in procuring them, I shall be so with pleasure. The sum I have to pay your father, is about sufficient to accomplish it, and shall be so applied if it is his pleasure. I shall be in Bedford during the last week of this month and the first of the next; you will of course visit us there or here, when we can make more particular arrangements. I have here the two best works on Natural Philosophy, and Astronomy, Hauy and Biot, which I have imported for you from Paris, knowing they were not to be had here. Present me affectionately to Mr. and Mrs. Eppes, and be assured of my warmest attachment to yourself.

Th. Jefferson.

Ave Atque Vale!

On July 2, 1826, when Jefferson lay dying on his unique alcove bed between his study and his bedroom he handed a little casket to his daughter, Martha Randolph, who sat beside him. On opening it after his death she found a piece of paper on which he had written a touching bit of poetry he had composed and addressed to her. It was his farewell letter to her. The "two seraphs . . . long shrouded in death" who awaited him were his wife and daughter Maria.

A Death-bed Adieu from Th. J. to M. R.

Life's visions are vanished, its dreams are no more;
Dear friends of my bosom, why bathed in tears?
I go to my fathers, I welcome the shore
Which crowns all my hopes or which buries my cares.
Then farewell, my dear, my lov'd daughter, adieu!
The last pang of life is in parting from you!
Two seraphs await me long shrouded in death;
I will bear them your love on my last parting breath.

206

$\mathcal{I}ndex$